I
HEAR
BLUEBIRDS

Dr. Shirl Brunell

VANTAGE PRESS
New York / Los Angeles / Chicago

Shirl Brunell

To my big brother

Cover photo of Dr. Brunell by Bob Burns
All other photos by Dr. Shirl Brunell
Editors: Georgia M. Daily
         Cathy Camhy
         Mike Sivilli
Summaries of this book have previously appeared in
Rural Arkansas Magazine and *Arkansas United Methodist*

FIRST EDITION

Published by Vantage Press, Inc.
516 West 34th Street, New York, New York 10001

Manufactured in the United States of America
ISBN: 0-533-07702-8

Library of Congress Catalog Card No.: 87-91743

Acknowledgments

My greatest appreciations go to my Mom for her gentleness, her incredible patience and unique understanding, and for teaching me to pay attention, to Demie Choue for teaching me all about the world of tiny creatures, to Georgia M. Daily for her phenomenal editing, and to Dr. Lawrence Zeleny for his encouragement, his extraordinary expertise, and for giving so generously of his time. And, Dad, thanks for molding my sense of humor.

Foreword

Ever since early colonial times, the bluebird has been one of North America's best loved birds. Its great beauty, its gentle and friendly manner, and its alluring song, especially during courtship, have endeared the bluebird to all whose souls are in any degree attuned to Nature. Because of these attributes, the bluebird, in early times, came to be a symbol of love, hope, and happiness. This symbolism has persisted throughout the years, and the bluebird today is mentioned more frequently than any other bird in America's romantic poetry and in the lyrics of our popular songs.

The late Frank M. Chapman of the American Museum of Natural History, one of America's foremost ornithologists, was moved to express his feelings poetically in his classic *Birds of Eastern North America*:

The bluebird's disposition is typical of all that is sweet and amiable. His song breathes of love; even his fall call-note—*tur-wee, tur-wee*—is soft and gentle. So associated is his voice with the birth and death of the seasons that to me his song is freighted with all the gladness of spring-time, while the sad notes of the birds passing southward tell me more plainly than the falling leaves that the year is dying.

In a similar mood, nature columnist Ruth Thomas, in describing the bluebird's song, once wrote:

Several other birds sing plaintive or wistful songs, but the bluebird's warble is sometimes a yearning, other times an all but unbearable ecstasy!

Bluebirds, unfortunately, have fallen into desperately hard times over the last half century, due in large part to unwise human decisions and activities. With rare exceptions, bluebirds nest and raise their young in small enclosures of some kind, usually cavities or old woodpecker holes in dead trees or wooden posts. Dead trees are now commonly cut away, and the old wooden fence posts are rapidly being replaced with metal posts, thus depriving the bluebirds of many of their former natural nesting sites. But the greatest insult of all to our bluebirds came with the unfortunate introduction of the house sparrow (also known as the English sparrow) and the European starling into North America from Europe during the last century. These foreign birds, in a remarkably short time, overran most of the continent. They are both cavity-nesters like the bluebird, and because of their large numbers and aggressive behavior, they usurp most of the nesting sites needed by the bluebirds and often kill the bluebirds with which they compete.

Unusually severe winters have also taken their toll on the bluebird population. Here again, the alien starlings have made matters worse by consuming a large part of the wild berry crop needed by the bluebirds to survive winter weather.

Thousands of concerned people throughout the United States and Canada, and even Bermuda, through the efforts of several organizations, have taken up the cause of the bluebird. They are helping by supplying the bluebirds with starling-proof nesting boxes to compensate for the shortage of available natural cavities, and by protecting the birds when possible during the nesting season. There is some evidence of a recovery in the bluebird population in many parts of the country during the past several years (1981–1986), probably due in part, at least, to human help. It is hoped that through these efforts, bluebirds will continue to increase and to bring joy to our children and grandchildren for many generations to come.

Dr. Shirl Brunell in this book describes in intricate detail her fascinating and heartwarming experiences in rescuing, hand-raising, and eventually releasing to the wild two five-day-old infant bluebirds. These tiny babies had been attacked, thrown out of their nest, and nearly killed by marauding house sparrows. Their three siblings had been killed outright or soon died as a result of this brutal assault.

The extreme rapport and affection that developed between these rescued bluebirds and their foster mother during the birds' lives, and the depth of feeling experienced by the human partner in this relationship, would be hard for me to understand and appreciate if I had not had very similar experiences years ago. One who has had experiences like this may find it difficult to accept the prevailing belief that birds are essentially automatons and that their behavior is guided by instinct alone. After all, in the final analysis, most human activities are instinctive, and for the most part, only intellectual pursuits have set us apart from the rest of the animal kingdom. We should remember that there is a vast difference between intelligence and wisdom. Perhaps some of the more humble of God's creatures have learned better than we have how to use their limited intelligence wisely.

Reading Shirl Brunell's book is truly an emotional experience. You may expect to smile, laugh, and shed more than a few tears as you follow the touching love affair between the author and her charming bluebird "foster children." And you will be filled with wonder and may ask yourself if we humans are really as superior to all the rest of God's creatures as our conceit has led us to believe. Shirl's true story as told so beautifully by her is a classic in American literature.

—Lawrence Zeleny
Founder, North American Bluebird Society

November 22, 1986

Prologue

Nesting boxes are everywhere. Really, there are too many. But they are for bluebirds, and there never can be too many bluebirds. The nesting box poles were set in concrete several years ago, and their placements have remained, making extra accommodations for titmice and chickadees. Regrettably, the dreaded house sparrow also makes himself at home. It was several years ago that a friend gave me my first two bluebird boxes for my birthday in April, but delivered them two months early so they would be available when the bluebirds arrived. I knew nothing about bluebirds. I thought they migrated to Brazil in the winter and returned to southern America to nest in the spring. Nevertheless, at noon on that cold winter's day in early February, I nailed my birthday presents on the fence in the field and the power pole off the front porch of my country home, and waited. At 2:00 p.m., two fuzzy, blue-winged, winter-coated, orange-breasted creatures came to inspect the apartments for rent.

I thought that was the way it worked. Put up a box and the birds come. Therefore, when that first pair of beauties arrived in two hours' time, I was not surprised. Very pleased, but not surprised.

Everyone I know who is knowledgeable about bluebirds was astonished that the birds found the boxes so quickly. Had they flown from Brazil in two hours? The teasing continues to this day. Now I know bluebirds in

"When a bird is shot, it is a mother or father, or sister or brother who dies."

Arkansas and Texas usually stay in the areas during the winter and do not migrate.

There was so much I had to learn about bluebirds. (I remember how delighted I was when I proudly balanced a new birdbath on a tree stump and watched the first bluebirds flock to my gift. At the time, I did not know bluebirds soak and float in their baths just like people. One glimpse through my dining room picture window at a little creature with wings spread out across the water catapulted me out of the house and across the patio to rescue what I thought was a drowning bluebird. While leaping across the den floor, I created emergency plans in my mind of how to do mouth-to-mouth resuscitation on a bird. I scared the little fellow half to death as I rounded the corner of the house and into view of the birdbath.) Yes, there was so much I had to learn about the bluebird—and over the past few years, I have. One fact I especially was glad to discover was that, as territorial as the bluebird is, three pairs can nest simultaneously and comfortably on the five acres surrounding my home.

In any event, it became my goal to improve my photographic skills and increase my experience with these little creatures. I would choose a time to follow the bluebird's development step by step in pictures. Maybe I could create a little picture book for children to browse through in my office.

As my love of this devoted, family oriented, magnificent little creature deepened, somehow it became more and more important to share my bluebird experiences with others, especially little boys with BB guns. Perhaps it would make a difference for a youngster to learn that birds travel in families and when a bird is shot, it is a mother or a father, or a sister or brother who dies. Perhaps a battered child brought to my office would take interest in the gentle nature of the bluebird, needing kinder things to think about. There are many reasons why I wanted to create a bluebird picture book.

Now the time seemed right. My experience with the bluebird was substantial and my competence with the camera I thought adequate.

In late winter, a bluebird pair selected the nesting box by the pumphouse, making their activities easily visible from my home. In the spring, the female gathered straw from my strawberry patch and eagerly carpeted her new home. Her mate stood guard and inspected her work. If a territorial enemy had disturbed her, he would have fought valiantly to protect his lady. Yet their distribution of housework did seem a bit typical. She flew full speed for three hours. He watched.

Within five days the floor of their home was filled

with five tiny time capsules, with bluebird secrets a million years old locked only temporarily inside. At the moment I had no idea that a combination of tragedy and nature gone wild would plunge me into the most intimate of all possible contact with the lives of these baby bluebirds.

DAY ONE

Monday

The parent bluebirds grew more vigilant. I grew more vigilant. Something was happening. Then I saw the mama peeking out of the nesting house door. She had an egg shell in her mouth. Her five babies were to meet the world—and me.

The parents and I have become good friends. They know I am not an enemy. They know me as the lady who works the strawberry patch, keeps their birdbath filled, and carries a camera attached to a three-legged pole. My rare peeks at their family of azure eggs are timed to miss their presence and are staged only to determine the number of babies to be hatched and to take a fast picture. At one point, I watch their departure, run for the ladder, scurry up, take a picture, scurry down, and run with the ladder all before they can fly to and from the farmer's garden across the valley.

Immediately after the bluebird parents take their babies' shell covering off into the distance to avoid attracting predators to their nesting site, I do my scurrying act. And there it is—the first baby, his head now in the world, his bottom still protected by his eggshell home. He looks as if he is sitting in a miniature tea cup, his tiny wings-to-be stretching out to the world for the first time. Even before his shell is shed, he cries squeakily for food, his little mouth opening to me—as the movement of his nesting box lid alerts him that I might be a parent bringing dinner.

The scene repeated itself, parent birds with egg shells and I with ladder and camera. One baby could not help another. Each had to peck its way to freedom from the inside out. Soon they would help each other in sharing their body warmth, but now it was every bird's peck for itself.

And suddenly there were three! The snap of the camera opened mouths and shutter simultaneously. I and my camera departed quickly, as parents, faithful in their feedings and nest cleaning, dutifully removed all refuse to a distance, again not to disclose the location of the new babies. In five hours, there were five offspring, hatched and insatiably hungry. What more could I have wanted for my birthday the coming Easter weekend?

DAYS TWO, THREE AND FOUR

Tuesday, Wednesday, and Thursday

Mouths are open. Eyes are closed. Hints of fuzz where feathers will grow are visible. How do such ungainly, scrawny little creatures ever acquire such phenomenal beauty? Where did the bluebird learn such devotion to his family and mate? Is it pure instinct that leads him through some ritual, or is it love? How do adults know one baby from another?

The books say parents know which baby was fed last even if the babies become rearranged in the parents' absence. Even human parents of identical twins cannot do that. Some say the baby most in need of food lifts its head the highest, signaling to the parent its greater need. These days are filled with feedings, house cleanings, and warmings of baby birds—while a lengthy lady stands on a tall ladder looking quickly through a lens.

DAY FIVE

Friday

A pesky pair of alien house sparrows keeps getting a little pushy. Many other nesting boxes are available and yet this couple seems to be interested in my picture story box with the nest of five babies.

House sparrows have been known to peck to death a bluebird parent in a nest as he tries to shield his young with his body. Then without conscience, the sparrow may build his own nest over the bluebird parent and his dead or dying nestlings. Or the kill may come outside the bluebird's home, leaving one adult against two to guard and feed alone. While the single parent is away foraging, the sparrows cruelly throw the defenseless bluebird babies out onto the ground, and then build their own nest on top of that of the bluebirds.

(Surely that immigrant fool did not know the destruction he was bringing to the bluebird when he took to heart the Shakespearean passage about the sparrow, and set a male and female free in America over a century ago. More were to follow. Killing of any kind always creates cringing in me. Yet, secretly I sometimes wish for a blizzard of bluebirds to come and painlessly wipe out the excessive house sparrow population. Other sparrow species are not the enemy; why must the alien house sparrow be so cruel?)

Several times, agitated tweetings of the adult bluebirds alerted me to the sparrows' presence. Several times, I have seen the sparrows on or near the nesting box, but the bluebirds' flying dives at them appeared adequate to contain the invaders' trespassings. Surely, the sparrows will tire of the game and move on to more welcome territory.

Meanwhile, I have become very proficient in my ladder, scurry, camera routine. Would that I were invisible, or the size of an ant, and could observe those five growing fledglings hour after hour, for as long as I choose. Little did I know that part of my wish shortly would come true.

.

DAY SIX

Saturday

A 6:30 a.m. trip to the barn brought greetings from mama bluebird, ready to sail from overhead to her babies' door with a juicy bite of food. I could hear from the distance the squeaky tweetings of her baby brood as her landing told that breakfast was about to be served. I smiled in response to the sound of fresh life, wondering what it would be like to eat a worm. A friend of mine did that once when we were four and five, and she seemed perfectly pleased with her accomplishment. I still remember my mother's grimace when I told her Carol Ann ate a worm.

No bluebird parents were visible on my return trip

from the barn, but the sparrows were. My mind told me the parent bluebirds were still foraging in the farmer's garden across the valley to the south. Their distant flyings routinely were from that direction. Otherwise, they hunt crickets, worms, and insects on the ground near the nesting box.

The sun's face was too low for picture taking and so my plan this Saturday morning was to make a trip into the city and, in the direct light of early afternoon, to take the next series of photos. At 9:00 a.m., I ran to the nesting box to shoo away the sparrows, wondering where the bluebird parents were. The sparrows moved away and I was satisfied all was safe.

At 10:00 a.m., with shopping list in hand, I backed my car out of the carport. The two sparrows were nearby, and there still was no sign of the bluebird parents. Chilled by the 35-degree weather, I sat and waited.

Twenty minutes passed and no bluebirds. Twice the sparrows came to the nesting box. Twice I jumped from the car to scatter them. Growing more anxious to leave, I thought it wise to see if a parent might be in the box, covering those tender babies with its body. Up with the ladder to take a quick peek. Five tiny babies snuggled head to tail in a tiny circle, all lifted hungry opened mouths in unison at me for food.

Where were those parents? Another fifteen minutes passed. With my own body growing colder and my mind reordering my priorities in order not to leave, I reached to turn the ignition key to return to the carport just as the male parent flew from the south and straight into the nest box door.

"Where have you been!" I fussed aloud as I started the engine, and headed for town.

Through the next two hours, somehow I could not

5

rest easy. There was something strange about the adult bluebirds' long absence. Finally I cut my list short and returned to monitor the situation.

As I eased up the driveway, the windshield framed the scene of the nesting box—and the dreaded deadly predicament that had drawn me home. The female sparrow hung from the door of the box and the male perched on the lid.

I ran screeching over the grassy knoll toward the bluebirds' home, put up the ladder and opened the lid.

The nest was empty. I listened for bluebirds. I looked for bluebirds. My mind shot through all possible explanations like lights across a scanner. Then I looked down.

Tiny, pitiful naked bodies were everywhere. One on the pump house roof was dead and bloody. Three others, still alive, but barely, were hidden here and there in the grass. The fifth was nowhere in sight. I gently gathered the three live baby birds to me and screamed to a neighbor for help. I searched for the fifth baby as the neighbor took the dead nestling for burial under the oak tree.

With tiny, cold lives tucked against my body, I walked tiptoe around and around the pole of the nesting box, still searching for number five. Then, realizing the three babies in my hand must be warmed and fed quickly, I hurried into my house.

I do not remember finding the hot water bottle. All I remember is sitting on the floor of my den staring at those nearly lifeless nestlings. I could not bear the warmth of my home, knowing that the last baby lay alone, either dead or waiting for death. Or, more hopefully, waiting for rescue from the cold. Again I ran. Again I tiptoed all around the nesting box—north and south, east and west.

And I found him. He was slumped behind the pump house, his little beak broken and bleeding. Tenderly, I lifted him to me, trying to be a giant cradle and praying for a miracle. Frantically, I rushed to rest him with the others on the warm water bottle.

I thumbed through my books and found an orphaned bluebird formula: ground meat or finely chopped liver, baby cereal, hard boiled egg yolk, codliver oil or bird vitamins, and milk, preferably powdered, all mashed together in a pasty consistency.

I stirred up a batch and, jaw clinched tightly, fed the little babies gently with a blunted toothpick, watching life struggling to return.

The baby with the broken beak seemed to fight the hardest. In the strange way the mind sometimes works, I thought of tomorrow, Easter Sunday, and wondered if an Easter egg might make the difference between life and death.

It is an old wives' tale that parent birds will not accept a fallen nestling back into the fold. Nevertheless, to return the birds to the nest seemed the thing to try, and so I held the now warmed and fed babies close to me and climbed back up the ladder.

As gently as a surgeon, I placed each, one by one, back in the cold, dark nest, questioning all the while if this was what Dr. Zeleny, the bluebird expert, would do. I thought of telephoning him. I thought of calling the North American Bluebird Society. I thought of calling the Audubon Society. I thought of calling the veterinarian. All I could do was back away and pray.

After 45 miserable minutes, and no parents in sight, I knew those four dependent, defenseless lives inside that dark wooden box stuck high up in the chilling air soon would die. For another 10 minutes I searched the grounds for evidence of a bluebird-sparrow struggle. While my back was turned, those dastardly sparrows returned, convincing me that now I must take whatever parental action was to be taken.

Tenderly I lifted up my young ones and returned to my nesting spot on the den floor of my home, where I sat and watched, and fed, and warmed four baby bluebirds covered to their chins with a tattered baby blanket that had warmed a tiny toy poodle once long ago.

Had I not known about the lifeless appearance of baby birds found outside the nest for whatever reason, I would have assumed these four tiny creatures to be dead, or beyond revival. Yet, they began to stir.

Life did not return easily. I breathed every struggling breath with them. Miniature hearts beat desperately through paper-thin skin. Agonizingly, I watched two more babies die. With gloves and shovel and tears, I buried the fragile little bodies pressed tightly together next to their first little brother under the huge protective oak tree.

And now there were two: one too small, one too injured. Soon surely there would be none.

The day labored on and I labored in my parent role, vigilant to any request for food. With an eye dropper turned slightly sideways so as not to run the tube far down the tiny throat, I offered each little mouth droplets of warm water. Each cried for more.

Knowing that baby birds require support for their fragile little bodies, I rolled a towel and tucked it just right to form a nest cup over the heating pad (which had replaced the hot water bottle). The heating pad itself was curved slightly by the sides of the shallow box. This allowed the bird its preferred slightly forward tilt over its underdeveloped foot structure and gave it rear end support.

It gave me a moment's pause, however, wondering what the world would think of this grownup lady responding with such total absorption to the challenge of trying to keep two obviously dying infant bluebirds alive by not merely feeding, but trying to catch the neat little sacked dropping each baby makes after being fed.

Maybe it was just my way of distracting myself from the tragedy that had just befallen this bluebird family and my apprehensions about the future of these two remaining orphans, especially the injured one who displayed such determination to live. Each bite of food took an act of special courage from him, obviously requiring enormous effort to force open and control his pitiful little beak, broken at the corner, his nostrils swollen with blood.

I watched him. I admired him, I felt a growing love, and I knew at that moment he must be given a royal name of strength.

This is a tough little bird, but this is moving too fast. Perhaps he will not make it through the night.

Hours passed and the day slowly died, but my brave injured baby bluebird and his little companion clung to life. What else could I do but wait and watch, feed... and pray?

The books say to feed orphaned birds from dawn to dark, from 7:00 a.m. to 7:00 p.m. Yet, at 8:30 p.m., these two orphans still ask for food. With each bite, their strength increases. They *did* go many hours without food. Why not feed them all they want?

The books also say that giving a wild creature a name tends to enhance unhealthy attachment. But I cannot continue to refer to the tough little fighter as the baby with the broken beak, and his little companion who tucks herself up against him as the smaller one. It is too confusing. I choose to name them and run the risk of attachment.

The smaller one seems like a girl, but I cannot say

why. Maybe because she is smaller. But little boys also can be frail.

The one with the broken beak seems like a boy, but, again, I cannot say why. Maybe because he is such a fighter. But little girls also can be courageous.

Who in history was a valiant fighter? Solomon, David, Samson? Samson, champion of the Israelites, known for his strength. Name a baby bird with a broken beak Samson? Anything fighting as hard as this little fellow deserves a regal name, and so, Samson it is. His little sister keeps tucking herself up against him. Samson and Baby Sister. Oh well, they probably will not survive the night anyway.

To get involved has risks. Not to get involved has risks. To do nothing has risks. One cannot get away from risks. The least I can do is run one night's risk of attachment.

DAY SEVEN

Sunday

Easter morning. Dare I go downstairs? Will I find life or death in my den this Easter morning?

The first tap of my foot on the hallway floor brought echoes of tweetings equalling a nest of ten. What a wonderful racket. What hungry little cries. Hurriedly, I warmed baby food in a shallow bowl under hot running water and collected a few drops of warm tap water in a cup. As I lifted the puppy blanket off the lady-made nest, Samson and Baby Sister were all mouths—as they were when there were five mouths down inside their real home.

Both babies gulped down water and, in less than forty-five seconds, the entire feeding session was complete. Quickly, Samson and Baby Sister drifted back into slumber, evidently Mother Nature's way of keeping her broods contented in the natural confinement of their nesting quarters.

Poor little Samson, the top of his beak is even more black and bruised this morning. But the break appears to be in the right corner only, and at least no more fresh blood appears.

In the last few hours of the morning, I have experimented with different feeding signals. Without question, whistling is unacceptable. Both babies cower in fear. "Twitit"—my imitation of the adult bluebird's call—does not arouse them. Snapping my finger is ineffective. The *ping!* sound of tapping a table knife on the floor tile seems to work best. But if they survive, in time there surely will be occasion to call them on the outside. Obviously, tapping a knife on the floor will not do. I want to find a signal that they can become conditioned to respond to under any circumstances.

How did my mama call my brother and me? How could I forget. *"Suppertime!"* My mama would tell me to go call my dad and brother for dinner, and she said I would go within hearing distance and, in singsong fashion, call out, "Sup-pa..time!" To this day, on my visits home, my mom teasingly announces mealtime with, "Suppatime!" This is what I will try.

The day is warmer than yesterday, with all its chilling gloom and tragedy. How can I handle feeding Samson and Baby Sister and attend an early afternoon Easter dinner? The invitation was accepted days ago and I want to go. Yet, I cannot take into the middle of my host's

Easter dinner these two gangly little membrane-skinned creatures who dooky at random and without etiquette over the sides of their bed after each meal.

Perhaps leaving them in the car parked in the warm sunshine would keep them comfortable enough. After all, their feeding only takes about a minute, and surely I can slip out and back before anyone misses me.

Sure enough, Samson and Baby Sister and I completed our first social engagement without incident. I imagined those two to be the only baby bluebirds on earth to ride in a car from country to city for Easter dinner. But this brings up another question: what do I do with two baby bluebirds when I go to work tomorrow? My breaks between appointments are scheduled once an hour.

I will think about it and make my decision in the morning. In the meantime, I am acting as if Samson's and Baby Sister's lives no longer are in jeopardy. But with my determination to make it so, these two babies will live and fly and be set free. Surely, my imagination tells me, they can be returned to the heavens from whence they came—a reasonable Easter wish, I think.

DAY EIGHT

Monday

I eased down the stairs with trepidation, but a bit more optimistic than I was the previous morning. As humans tend to do during moments of apprehension, I held my breath.

"Sup-pa-time," I sang out lightly as my foot met the

hallway. Again, the welcome racket. I want to believe Samson and Baby Sister already are responding to my calls, but the truth is, I know they respond to any noise that promises food. Now I am convinced Samson and Baby Sister are going to live. Besides sickness, what else can harm them? Secretly, all these hours I have believed there was no question but that they would live.

This morning, the straggly hair on the top of their heads is even longer and a little thicker. I am not sure what the dark ridges are down their backs and over their eyebrows, very visible under their skin. For the most part, their eyes remain closed, but if open at all, they do not seem to focus. Evidently, they are responsive primarily to light. Samson's little nostril does not appear quite as puffy this morning, but his beak remains as bent in the corner. Having no experience with baby birds with broken beaks, I do not know if his beak will straighten out on its own.

This raises another question. What do bluebird parents do about food collecting at the corners of their babies' mouths? Surely, bug food does not collect and get crusty as the cereal formula does, especially in the area of Samson's broken beak. Very gently soaking and washing the hardened food with a warm cloth seems to help, and neither baby seems to mind.

Gradually, I have worked toward the goal of extending feedings to hourly intervals, attempting to condition Samson and Baby Sister to the schedule that they will have to submit to at my office. My decision is to take the shallow box with their nest and food supply and keep them in the storage room off the hall next to my office. That way, I can keep them warmed with the heating pad and can tend to them between appointments.

My secretary smiled at me in quiet resignation as

she saw what I was carrying into the storage room, tactfully tolerating one more predicament I had managed to get myself into. She is as patient with me as I am with Samson and Baby Sister and other little creatures.

The routine went well through the day. Only once did someone mention quizzically he thought he heard baby birds. Innocently, I passed it off as a phenomenon of the springtime.

In the early evening, a fellow bluebird lover brought a supply of more lean ground meat, a strip of calf's liver, some bird vitamins, and a container of long wiggly fishing worms. All of these ingredients went into a fresh batch of baby bluebird food.

Making hash out of a leathery strip of liver is not a lot of fun, and cutting a worm in two and watching each end squirm off in different directions is positively unnerving. I am not a fisherperson and will go to ridiculous lengths to avoid killing any creature. I told myself that surely after a couple of dozen worm feedings, I would become desensitized. I am not sure that is true, but I have become more skilled at being on target with my eyes closed and more resigned to accepting one little creature's death if another is to live. The books suggest providing food variety so orphan nestlings do not get bored and refuse to eat. I cannot imagine my two refusing to eat. All sorts of berries and crickets are recommended as sources of nourishment. Crickets! Uh-oh. I know what that means. First I will have to graduate from worms.

DAY NINE

Tuesday

Colonies of crickets chased me all night. I told Samson and Baby Sister about it. They squealed for food. It is amazing how much change just one night can bring. These birdies were noticeably naked when I first took them in two days ago. Now, this third day, a prickly appearance is visible all over them, a hint of pinfeathers perhaps.

The day was completed without incident. Baby care is becoming more routine: warm food, whack worm, feed, tuck baby in to sleep. Actually, both babies seem to prefer the homemade meal with only a taste of worm. Temporarily, at least, this reduces the number of worm deaths involved.

Samson and Baby Sister gradually are growing more active. Every spare moment, I just sit and study these two tiny gawky creatures on my den floor. Almost from hour to hour, there is some subtle developmental accomplishment. Once a movement occurs, it tends to repeat, leading to the acquisition of a skill. By last feeding this evening, both babies fairly well had mastered reaching and scratching with their beaks, especially under their wings. Samson's slightly sturdier body gives him a slight advantage, but he is cautious not to put much pressure on the end of his bill.

When tucked up close to Samson, Baby Sister has a characteristic way of extending her neck to sleep. Samson will do this too, periodically. Both are very sensitive to noise and so I keep conversations, television, the phone ring, and other activities at a low volume.

Sometimes one of them tumbles over in the nest and has great difficulty righting itself. Usually I help support its little body until it crawls back to an upright position. The exercise is good, I think, but such a tumble would be unlikely in a nest of five. Perhaps I do not have the nest cupped sufficiently as a bed for only two. For certain, one problem must be corrected. Samson's and Baby Sister's claws are catching more and more on the towel sheet and the blanket covering. I must find a more suitable material.

DAY TEN

Wednesday

Samson and Baby Sister sometimes leave a little prize in my absence, creating the need to change the nest bed regularly. Several brands of paper towels were purchased at the store early this morning. One of the more expensive tightly woven paper towels seems to work best. Should a claw get badly caught, the material could be torn apart to free the tiny toenail. If a slight catch occurs, a small lift on the baby's body in the direction of its body tilt tends to encourage the little bird to release its claw. (If lifted in the opposite direction, the baby tends to grasp more tightly, undoubtedly an early response that eventually will lead to perching.)

This morning Samson and Baby Sister are opening their eyes more often. How much they can see is questionable, but momentarily, both seem to study light changes. Fuzzy hair growth is more visible down their spines and on their heads. Ribbing which eventually will become feathers is evident on their wings. Hints of tail feathers appeared almost overnight.

All has gone well this the tenth day of my baby bluebirds' lives. Foster parenting does have its problems, but caring for them is a joy.

DAY ELEVEN

Thursday

With warm baby food and a few drops of water in hand, I peeked under the covering from which squeaky tweetings could be heard. What a burst of chirping! When I offered food, however, both babies ducked back fearfully. Evidently, their focusing ability has improved significantly overnight. Until they understand what my hand is all about, I must remember to approach them more slowly. After all, I do want the time to come when they will sit on my hand and eat.

Tiny side-of-rib feathers are taking shape and babyfine white pinfeathers about a sixteenth to an eighth of an inch long are peeking through, especially on Samson's and Baby Sister's legs. All of the initial dark ridges under the skin are the main places of fuzz and pinfeather growth. Changes are visible even from morning to evening, and especially overnight.

It is becoming a part of my evening to sit by Samson and Baby Sister and study them before tuck-in time. Both babies now spend more time awake and, at moments, are noticeably more active. Many of their movements appear to be infantile grooming responses that, in time, will lead to self-care. Grooming must be totally instinctive, as they never have witnessed this behavior, certainly not in me. At one point, Samson suddenly stretched his body high, extended his wings as far as they would reach and fluttered them vigorously for several seconds, then nestled down in his bed, Baby Sister snuggling up tightly against his side. They tolerate each other so well. I wonder if my brother and I tolerated each other equally well. In looking back, it seems so.

DAY TWELVE

Friday

Samson and Baby Sister now are able to focus quite well. Their little eyes follow my movements. Yet, as I have noticed birds do in the wild, often they tend to hold very still and only move their eyes. This behavior must be a built-in protective response that keeps them from revealing their whereabouts to a predator.

Last spring, for example, just as I was about to spray a fruit tree, I looked up just in time to spot a nest of blue jays tucked down in the fork of the trunk. For fifteen minutes or more, I had mixed solutions and prepared hoses and made quite a commotion not five feet below them but they remained motionless. Except for the motion of their eyes, they appeared inanimate. I walked around and around the tree, gathering up my hose and spraying materials, yet those fledging blue jays held as still as the bark on the tree.

Both Samson and Baby Sister are now covered fairly well in stubby feathering or baby down, but their little bottoms and around their ears and the center of their chests are still quite bare and their necks only have patchy feathering. Both babies can scratch fairly well under their heads with their feet, leaving prickly pinfeather stubs in their bed. Surely itching urges some of the scratching, evidently Mother Nature's way again of teaching her offspring how to groom.

I usually devote Fridays to paper work or out-of-office duties and my country home, but this day has been spent with Samson and Baby Sister.

Evenings with my tiny friends have become so special. More and more, I find myself talking to them—and it seems perfectly natural. Talking to babies is what mamas do—and now that I am a mama, that is what I do. At this point, I believe I could pick Samson and Baby Sister out of a hundred baby bluebirds. Of course, Samson's broken beak would give him away. Yet, even if that were not true, baby birds have distinct personalities, as I learned some time ago.

Several years back, it had been a record-breaking summer of heat and drought and, in addition to other things, it resulted in the stunted growth in the development of five bluebird babies in a nesting box off my front drive. Routinely in the past, my bluebird boxes have been vacated no later than the 17th day, but the parents of these worked from 6:00 in the morning until after 8:00 at night trying to coax their 18-day-old fledglings from their home.

The first two babies finally made it to the protection of the trees overhead, but the last three scarcely could fly five feet. They managed to flutter to the ground, but could not lift off, leaving them vulnerable to predators. For two and one-half days, I worked with the three immature birds, hour after hour lifting them onto places of safety, fearing a stalking cat often seen nearby.

Each baby had a unique personality. One of them, when lifted onto a branch, immediately went to sleep. Another would run up the branch and call for his parents, and the last would chew me out in no uncertain terms, demanding to be put down, and the moment he was placed on a branch, off he would go, trying to fly again but only succeeding in fluttering to the ground and back into a position of danger.

Perhaps every creature that has ever lived has had a distinct personality. I know it is increasingly so with Samson and Baby Sister.

DAY THIRTEEN

Saturday

Samson and Baby Sister met me this morning standing straight up, their prickly necks extended. (When drawn down close in their beds, they look like fuzzy little soft stuffed toys. However, when feeding time comes, they look like miniature buzzards and their appetites match. Out of respect, I kept my thoughts to myself.)

I know that I must begin to vary their diet and offer insects and crickets for example. This aversive thought was wandering back and forth, in and out of my consciousness, as I began cleaning the kitchen, when a cricket, commonly seen in the country, ran across the sink behind the faucets. With a dinner knife, I whacked that cricket so hard there was little left to feed a baby bird. Perhaps

I was thinking that if I smacked him hard enough he would not suffer. I know this will not do. Somehow I must be brave enough to tap the cricket on the head with just enough strength to knock him out. Then, without gagging, I *will* feed him to Samson and Baby Sister.

Plans for an aviary in the yard are taking shape in my mind. I purchased lumber, nails, and screening this afternoon and began construction of one wall. But how will the protected freedom within the aviary adequately teach Samson and Baby Sister about danger? My thoughts cover this conflict repeatedly. I am convinced my birdchildren must be significantly more mature and independent than other fledglings before they are freed. Practice sessions hopefully will solve this problem.

DAY FOURTEEN

Sunday

An interesting change in sounds came from the nest this morning. Intentionally, I delayed feeding to study chirping differences—sounds noticeably like that of the adult bluebird. It is my understanding that baby birds imitate parent sounds, but after all this time, it is doubtful that they "remember" their parents' voices, and I certainly have not been chirping around the house, at least not to my knowledge. Yet, Samson and Baby Sister are approximating the adult "twitit".

Both babies display improved coordination almost from hour to hour and these past 24 have almost completed Samson's and Baby Sister's body coverings.

In the wild, some parents bring their babies out of the nest on the 15th day, and this is day number 14. Of course, those nestlings have parents to protect them on the outside. These babies would not last an hour on their own.

Adult bluebirds are showing interest in the nesting box a hundred yards to the northeast of the pump house box where my two were born. This pleases me and makes me wonder if by chance they would adopt my orphans as bluebirds have been known to do.

DAYS FIFTEEN, SIXTEEN AND SEVENTEEN

Monday

Today my secretary brought a piece of curved plastic mesh to place over the nest to keep the weight of the blanket off Samson's and Baby Sister's heads. The covering likewise helps contain them while allowing them freedom of movement.

During a feeding, however, I found Samson out from under the mesh and up on the outer edge of his bed. There he sat proudly looking up at me as if to say "Hi, Mama, look where I am," reminding me of a baby boy about to climb out of his crib.

Fussing at him did not seem like the thing to do. Correcting the situation seemed more appropriate, and so, with baby birds next to me in the car seat, later in the evening we rode together to town to buy a bird cage.

Tuesday

Samson, Baby Sister, and I experimented awhile this morning with last night's purchase. Neither of them likes the sound made by any object touching the metal bars. Even a button makes the whole cage reverberate. Latching the door sets both babies quivering and cowering. I must wait and work with them before dropping them in and carrying them to work in this new contraption. Meanwhile I will surround their baby bed with boxes at the office to provide a barrier should either try to crawl out of the nest.

Wednesday

Early this morning, I arranged Samson's and Baby Sister's nest on the floor of the little carrying cage. Feedings are going well enough in their new home, but it takes considerable contortions for me to get my arm in to feed and the other arm in in time to catch baby bird droppings, all the while trying not to scrape the metal bars. By work time, both babies seemed contented enough and so I decided to leave them in the little cage, covered by a towel between feedings. The decision was a good one. Twice in late afternoon I found Samson outside his bed and up in the corner of the cage.

Through the evening, Samson and Baby Sister were very active, seemingly resigned to their new quarters. I rewarded each with a raisin. Neither showed much interest. They knew it was not a cricket.

DAY EIGHTEEN

Thursday

Neither Samson nor Baby Sister has been interested in food early or late today. This is something new. I suspect the continued confinement is taking its toll. Perhaps a larger cage will help—until the aviary is completed. Under normal circumstances, Samson's and Baby Sister's mom and dad would be teaching them about the ways of the wilds and Mother Nature's gifts and risks. And if they were not already in the trees, this would be the day they would set sail. Undoubtedly, my babies' development at this point is comparable to other bluebird fledglings.

However, once released, bluebird babies learn very rapidly to fend for themselves, although under parental protection all the while. Each new nest, usually of four to six offspring, is integrated into the existing family and all stay together until deep into the following winter when separation for pairing and mating occurs. In a week from now, free fledglings would be noticeably independent of parent feedings.

In a week from now, my babies still will be noticeably dependent. I must work with them to teach them to come to me for food and then to make food available for them to seek on their own. Perhaps once they are freed, any delay in Samson's and Baby Sister's development will be overcome rapidly enough.

A pair of bluebird adults has been inspecting a box north of the little barn. Would that they would adopt Samson and Baby Sister, or at least show them skills this particular mama cannot teach. My first free day, I will place my two close by in the yard and see if those adults show any interest. I do not know what I will do if they do, but I must try.

The notion about the risks of getting involved, of not getting involved, or of doing nothing has become even more important to me in caring for Samson and Baby Sister, perhaps because it is part of what keeps me going and answers so many riddles for me, and perhaps because it is such an important part of my work. The source of pain for so many individuals with whom I work evolves out of the unfortunate belief that it is possible to choose a life's path that is free of risks. Then, when the pain comes, they conclude they chose the wrong path, and from there, create their own captivity in a self-styled cage that, with certainty, renders them casualties of their own feelings of anger and anguish.

In a therapy group this evening, I felt the need to discuss this issue, wanting to share Samson and Baby Sister, feeling so full of the joy that has grown out of tragedy and the risk of involvement. At the end of the discussion, in the softly lit, quieted room, I unlatched the little cage. Samson flew up to my sleeve and Baby Sister hopped out and onto my pants leg. One member whispered, *"Real, live bluebirds!"* Those endearing tiny beings pushed home the point my words struggled to make.

DAY NINETEEN

Friday

Samson is so eager to fly. It hurts me to hold him back. Hopefully, the larger cage will help, at least temporarily. Gently, I eased Samson and Baby Sister onto the floor of their new quarters. Immediately, Samson was off to explore. The doweling rods used for perches obviously were too high. I lowered one and placed Samson on it and, in an instant, he understood its purpose. Baby Sister roamed the cage floor, then sat in a corner and groomed herself.

It is late evening and Samson has become a little master at perching. Baby Sister is more retiring and tends to stay close to a corner but still on the floor, pushing up against the side of the cage, her little face a bit forlorn, a bit sad, looking out. Does she feel lost in the spaciousness, away from big brother's side?

Neither baby has returned to the nest bed. During the last feeding, Samson jumped onto my finger and hung on tightly, then hopped to my sleeve. While I was cornering Samson, Baby Sister bounced out of the open door and jumped up on my lap. Baby bluebirds all over me.

At nightfall, Baby Sister was huddled against the corner by the door unable to reach her big brother. In the way that nature works, Samson will not stay back for his little sibling. She has to progress to him. This sad sight prompted me to place both back in the baby cage in hopes they would sleep side by side. I have observed other fledglings do that on branches high above, their little bottoms resembling a cluster of pine cones. Whether such an alignment is an expression of affection, baby bluebirds' way of keeping warm, a return to an arrangement learned in the nest, or simply instinctive, I do not know. I prefer to think it is the first.

A late peek in the little cage showed Samson sleeping on the little perch and Baby Sister huddled close beneath him on the paper below. My babies are out of their nest forever, but are not yet free.

DAY TWENTY

Saturday

As I write this, Samson is staring me down, as if to say, "How long are you going to do this to me?" Baby Sister is grooming herself. Re-entry into the large cage this morning produced minimum activity. Samson received his food, moved to a high perch, to which now he readily can fly, and then sat inert and quiet. Baby Sister took her food, then sat on the floor of the cage pressed against the wire and went to sleep staring out the window of the sunken living room below. It is heartbreaking to have to cage these precious freedom-loving creatures.

Their occasional listlessness probably is indicative of why some animals raised in captivity do not thrive. Their entire mood is subject to alteration. Either they can submit to an enclosed existence in exchange for longer life, or can be turned free to face certain death in exchange for a few flights of freedom.

I wished I could explain to Samson and Baby Sister that I would create as much safe freedom for them as I knew how, and proved it by working all day on the walls of their aviary to be assembled in my yard.

In the late half of the afternoon, while constructing

27

the end wall with the door, I noticed an adult bluebird pair feeding on the ridge about seventy-five yards away. They have claimed the box in an open clearing straight to the north of my house and a hundred paces from Samson's and Baby Sister's original home. It crosses my mind that this pair could be my orphans' parents, although it is doubtful.

The weather was cold and wet, and yet for a moment the drizzling rain ceased. Quickly, I went for my babies, transferred them into the small carrying cage, and walked slowly toward the trees where the adult bluebirds were perched. As I placed Samson and Baby Sister on the ground close by and stepped back, the little ones continued their chirping briefly—then became quiet and stared wide-eyed in the direction of the adults who began chirping loudly and rapidly. I wished that their sounds were in response to my babies, but in truth, I believe they were warning some starlings to move out of their territory, which the starlings did shortly. The adults then continued to forage for food, but remained silent. The returning misty rain forced me and my two orphans back indoors.

DAY TWENTY-ONE

Sunday

This is the morning I have been dreading. This is the day Big Mama *will* give crickets to baby birds. I have a container full of the scratchy critters. I can see them through the wire mesh on the side of the box. This must be the way Roman guards felt, about to throw the Christians to the lions.

"I *am* in control of this situation," I told Samson and Baby Sister shakily. They stared at me quizzically.

Slowly I rotated the box top to align the lid and container holes. With dinner knife in hand, I cringingly waited for a cricket to crawl out of the opening. A head peeked out and studied its future. I explained to him that because he has no nerve endings, he surely could not experience pain. He showed no acknowledgment. I explained further. I told him I would clunk him so quickly he would never know what hit him—and what happened after that would be wonderful. It would be like an organ transplant; it would be like giving his heart so another being could live.

Unimpressed, the cricket continued to rotate his feelers in the air, then suddenly bolted out of the starting gate and ran as if he knew his life depended on it.

He dropped to the floor and off he went, with me the knife-armed giant in hot pursuit. Around the cage he scurried in search of cracks for cover, with me on my knees after him, thunking and whacking the knife at his every hop. It sounded like a native drum beat announcing war.

I thunked my way back around the cage, as Samson and Baby Sister stared in wide-eyed wonderment at this incredible scene, and was met by a cavalry of crickets.

I had left the box hole open and half of the colony had escaped. With a whack whack here and a whack whack there and here whack, there whack, everywhere a whack whack, I left cricket carcasses lying everywhere.

Finally, with a toothpick of homemade food, I lightly touched one of the immobilized bodies and it adhered easily to the pasty consistency.

Gagging the call of "suppatime," I aimed the feast gingerly toward Samson and in one big gulp, down it went. Then a meal for Baby Sister and another for Samson. If they were satisfied, I was satisfied, I chokingly concluded to myself. I placed the remaining dead bodies on the cage floor, hoping Samson and Baby Sister would pursue the morsels on their own. But when I returned for the afternoon feeding, the corpses were still there.

Determined to work on this goal, I held the food slightly away from each baby, requiring each to display some sign of independent movement in the direction of the food before being fed. I felt cruel, listening to their squeaky hungry cries as I teased them with their supper. This one procedure took over an hour per infant. Surprisingly, Baby Sister came to me better than Samson who has been more aggressive all along. All along, though, she has tried to get out of the open door to me, while I attend to Samson.

For the most part, both have trained me to give them water, and each will take repeated droplets. A hand reach per drop from cup to mouth. It seems like a game. Neither will accept water from the dropper held continuously overhead. They respond to a new hand approach and to the question, "Want some water?" with a baby cry and then a reach for the dropper.

Weeks later, I was to learn from Dr. Larry Zeleny that using an eye dropper is dangerous. Liquid can get trapped in the baby's lung, leading to immediate death. As he pointed out, fortunately, I proceeded so cautiously that in this case the procedure worked. I would never take such a risk again, as the bird's food provides sufficient moisture, although if desired it is acceptable to dampen it first.

This day Baby Sister learned to perch and to fly to the higher perch which Samson pretty much has made his home. Once on this homemade branch, she found her place next to Samson. Her happy chatter expressed her

30

delight as she nestled against him. Slowly she inched him over to the side of the cage until he could move no farther. This sweet scene followed me into sleep.

DAYS TWENTY-TWO THROUGH TWENTY-SEVEN

Monday

Two hours of withholding food yesterday until each bird showed independent movement brought some reward this morning. Baby Sister flew to the wire to meet me, and Samson took half a step in my direction. Both continue to flutter their wings in anticipation of mealtime, just as nestlings this age do in response to their parents.

I placed the large cage in my van for transportation to work. In my rear view mirror, I could see Samson and Baby Sister stretched high to see the sights out the windows. They were the tourists, and I the tour guide. I described points of interest along the way, waving my arms right and then left for emphasis. I must have traveled at least three miles before I realized I was gibbering a narrative in their behalf. I felt a slow blush of embarrassment as I noticed a motorist studying me curiously.

Tuesday

What a racket! The enthusiasm of their welcome does not match the size of these little creatures. I wondered what humans might learn from this about relationships. It would be so easy to forget the idea of ever freeing Samson and Baby Sister, as the nourishment of their greeting is so addictive. I talk sweetly to them and they talk back even more sweetly. I am discovering all the myths and legends about the bluebird are true. Their presence in my home creates a glow and a sense of magic. They do possess great healing power and confirm the story that I need not look along any other latitude or longitude to find the meridian of happiness on my side of the rainbow. The bluebird mirrors all that is soft, that is gentle, that is sweet, that is loving—and, like the rainbow, reflects a promise, the promise of spring's rebirth and winter's passage.

My mind asks why these marvelous little friends had to come into my life in such a tragic way. Seeing those babies lying lifeless on the cold ground was pure pain. Seeing these babies in my home is pure joy. Does pure joy ever exist without being framed in a background of pain?

Samson's and Baby Sister's clamorings broke through my reveries, telling me I had stood over the kitchen sink warming their food and staring blankly out the window long enough. Typical kids, I smiled, as I indulged myself in one more thought, wondering if all the youth of the world wanted attention.

This day showed excellent results of training Samson and Baby Sister to come to me for food. Both have done very well for the few hours invested. I concluded my babies were exceptionally bright. Typical parent.

During group therapy this evening, show and tell brought a little comedy. Samson crawled up my arm onto my shoulder and from there he sat on my head. The room filled with hushed giggles. He then made his first distant flight across the room onto a hanging lamp. He beamed with pride. Baby Sister crawled onto my sleeve and hung on tightly, the more retiring little being that she is, seemingly wanting to get close to her mama among the stares of so many big creatures. With a loving grasp, I held Baby Sister in one hand as I gathered up Samson in the other. As I returned them to the little cage and whispered, "You're wonderful," someone whispered, *"Why don't we say that to our kids?"*

Wednesday

Tonight I sat by the railroad tracks talking to a teenager with whom I have been working for months.

His heart hurt from his "nose-too-large to his feet-too-big," as he put it. He talked a while and I listened. Then I talked awhile and he listened.

With the quiet wisdom of the shaman he asked me to create images of hope in his head that might compete with the scenes he kept seeing of his father slapping his frail little mother. Already I had taught this wise young man about imagery. Already he understood how thinking consists of seeing in pictures and largely is governed by what we say to ourselves in the form of subvocal speech.

The boy knew leaving home would give him some relief, but his mother was dying of cancer and his father's drinking was getting out of hand. Despair bathed his demeanor and his young face looked old. In whispers he pleaded for hope. In whispers I told him about involvement. I filled his head and heart full of Samson and Baby Sister and the risks I had taken of getting involved. As the imagery of the legendary bluebird began to saturate his soul, his back began to straighten. He is such a fine and sensitive boy and I told him so. He will be a very productive citizen and I would be proud to have him for my son and I told him this, too. His jumping up so quickly and throwing his arms in the air startled me.

"I see Samson! He's learning to fly, so will I." He smiled slightly at his poetic words, adding more seriously as he turned to walk away. "Running away would mean not getting involved—and that's the worst risk of all." He paused and kissed me on the cheek as lightly as a bluebird.

Thursday

Samson and Baby Sister met me hungry and very wide awake. All feedings now are withheld until they seek food on their own. Both came to me within ten minutes this morning. At times, both ask for more and more water. Like any infant, sometimes they continue to fuss even if their tummies are full. If they get too much, they simply shake their heads vigorously and sling out any excess food and water like a baby rebelling at broccoli. To reinforce how well Samson came to me, I gave him an extra half of a worm, and after filling up on water, he did the characteristic head shaking and out came both worm and water. The worm stuck against the cage corner post, then fell to the floor. In unison, Samson and I studied the worm, watched its fall to the floor, then looked at each other. I laughed and wondered if baby birds giggle.

After work this evening I picked up some of Samson's and Baby Sister's first pictures. It is difficult to believe they ever were so tiny and helpless and featherless, now that both are so full of play and curiosity and are covered with beautiful blue feathers and baby down.

Friday

Office landscaping duties today dictated that I take my little pickup truck to town, demanding again that Samson and Baby Sister be returned to the tiny cage. Both were noticeably disturbed by the confinement. Initially setting them in the open office window where they could see my activities seemed to soothe their stress sufficiently. Early in the afternoon, while reworking a walkway, I lifted a stepping stone and a huge worm lifted his head at me. As quickly as I had whacked that first cricket in my kitchen, "Suppatime!" popped out of my mouth.

How I have changed, I thought.

Catching that worm now seemed instinctive. I laid the feast in front of Samson on the cage floor and waited, watching him as he watched the worm. He showed some slight interest and pecked at it a little but did not pick it up. As yet, he has not taken any food from the front of his beak, appearing bothered by any material on the end of it.

I praised him enthusiastically, telling him his attempts were grand and that I knew he would learn. He turned his attention to me, asking to be fed.

By the end of my labors, the day had lingered too long for Samson and Baby Sister, imprisoned in the miniature metal cell. I promised them in the noisy truck on the trip home I would never do this to them again.

In keeping with the researchers' descriptions of deteriorating behavior in species under continued stressful conditions, Samson and Baby Sister got down on the cage floor and rotated mechanically around and around in circles, crying and bumping into walls and each other in agitated confusion. Their relief when released back in the large cage was so visible it made me want to cry.

As an apology, I moved the van out under the trees where they could visit with the bluebird adults and other little winged beings in the forest, and stocked their cage with mulberry branches to play on. They seemed happy to accept my apology, and, more happily, I thanked them.

Saturday

Rather than prepare food immediately for Samson and Baby Sister, I waited an extra hour in hopes they would be hungry enough to seek nourishment more independently. And sure enough, yesterday's practice was sufficient preparation for Samson. I knocked a cricket in the head just hard enough to daze it and dropped it in the cage. Immediately, Samson was on the floor and pecking in its direction. Like an Indian on the warpath in the old Western movies, he raucously sounded his warning before devouring it. Following this success, I dropped a wiggling worm on the floor and Samson paraded around it again noisily signaling his intentions, and after only a pair of pecks, he popped it proudly down his throat.

I, too, felt like squealing. My little boy had taken his first major step toward freedom.

Baby Sister, perturbed at the neglect, was offering an ostrich-sized tantrum overhead. As I called her to the wire for a worm, Samson was so full of himself, he flew up and sat on Baby Sister's head and took the worm for himself before she could get to it. Half-heartedly, I tried to fuss at Samson, but giggled instead. I am sure this is why parents let so many questionable behaviors go uncorrected. Giggling renders them powerless.

Now Samson was full enough to leave Baby Sister to my attention, but she would not be enticed by the squirmy worm set before her. She continued to cry babyishly, and so I decided to take her training in a different direction temporarily. I closed all the van windows and the large door and opened the cage door. It is time also to begin training my baby bluebirds to hold onto my hand to eat, and I knew Baby Sister would come to me if given the chance. I must make certain both will come to me if necessary once they are freed.

By the end of the day, Samson was proficient in seeking food on his own, and both easily will eat from my hand. At one point, Samson ducked his head in the water bowl as if to drink, but he did not know how to scoop up the liquid. Perhaps that will be his next accomplishment.

My toddlers are developing well. Most developmental milestones for Samson continue to precede Baby Sister's by approximately one day. It is a mystery to me if he was first in the birth order. It is true that Samson and Baby Sister appeared ever so slightly larger than the two baby birds that died on the water bottle that first day. All of this tells me how much more I have to learn about my little blue-feathered friends.

I whistled tunes and sang calls to them in the distance as I cut out screens for the walls of their aviary. They sang back.

DAY TWENTY-EIGHT

Sunday

I worked today like a true mama bird building her nest . . . and finished the aviary. It would have been easier if I had painted the lumber before constructing and screening in the walls. There are too many awkward angles and tight spots for a paint brush to reach.

Another delay came when I covered the walls with screen wire instead of the larger-holed hardware cloth. Once the screen was in place, I worried that baby bird claws might hang on the finer mesh of the screening. It was doubtful, but I could not run any risk of injury, and so, I turned the walls inside out and added a layer of hardware cloth on the interior. A wire floor, covered with grass and dirt, was included to prevent any foreign creature from tunneling under the walls. Gophers maneuver their way across my property periodically, and it would be easy enough for one of them to meander into the middle of the aviary floor. Holes drilled in the floor two-by-fours allowed stakes to be driven into the ground to stabilize the little structure. With metal plates holding one wall to another, and a strip of tar paper covering part of one side and one end of the roof, the baby bird building was completed. I wondered if all mama birds felt as excited as I.

Closer to freedom, I thought as I carried Samson and Baby Sister in the tiny cage to their new home, singing, "Ooo, do-I-have-a-surprise-for-you!" the way my mother used to do for my brother and me. Immediately Samson found the higher perch. Immediately, Baby Sister found her place next to Samson. Such wide eyes. Such chatter. I do not know who was more excited, they or I.

"I had dreams of baby bluebirds playing all over me. That came true today."

Their first interest was in the nylon string anchoring the perches to the wire. They pulled and tugged on it as if it were a ten-inch worm. Freeing crickets in the aviary told me the screen wire/hardware cloth combination was ideal. The screen prevents the crickets' escape from the aviary territory, but the large hardware cloth allows some temporary protection. As a cricket runs in and out of the protected area, my babies gain practice pursuing prey.

A cricket clamoring for cover caught Samson's eye and onto the ground he went, where he discovered a whole

"They were inseparable . . . I found Samson and Baby Sister nearing sleep, snuggled together on the highest perch under the rooftop."

new world of objects to pull and peck. Baby Sister's interest followed Samson's and together they journeyed, exploring all ground paths in their new home. Not one blade of grass was left uninspected.

It was wonderful watching them wander freely but, in time, I began to worry. Are they learning to stay on the ground too long?

Candi and Duet, both part bird dog, lie one foot outside the screen wire. They roam free and have a lot of the wilderness left in them. I have trained them to tolerate baby chickens fairly well, but they play at chasing birds on the ground below the feeders in front of my home. They, too, are loved and could not be contained long enough significantly to reduce the risks. Sometimes the number of risks that crosses my mind seems overwhelming.

40

From the time of the first flight of my nestlings years ago, I have had dreams of baby bluebirds playing all over me. That came true today. Baby birds pulled at my pockets, chased each other back and forth across my shoulders, perched on my boot tops, pulled at the fray on my shorts, played in my hair, sat on my collar, and gave me butterfly kisses with their soft wings against my cheeks. What clean sweet smells of baby down they have, and how considerate they are! They move momentarily to a perch to make a bird dropping, then hop back to me as I sit on a little homemade stool in the middle of their new home. When eating from my hand, they stretch their little bottoms far enough over the side to make sure their droppings miss me.

This day brought two more successes. Samson drank water on his own and Baby Sister, after numerous failures, finally captured her first cricket. In her chase for crickets, she squeals too long and pecks indiscriminately at the wrong objects. An urge to pick her up and hug her comes over me when she sweetly squeaks her warning to a cricket, then boldly captures a blade of grass.

In the darkening evening, I found Samson and Baby Sister nearing sleep, snuggled together on the highest perch under the roof top and on the end closest to the unscreened wall. This placed them about eight inches from me and as high as my nose.

When I whispered bedtime expressions to them, their cooing conveyed to me their contentment with their new little castle.

DAYS TWENTY-NINE THROUGH THIRTY-TWO

Monday

Placing them back in the van cage to return to my office this morning was as disturbing to me as it was to Samson and Baby Sister. Their unhappy ritualistic behavior, followed by listlessness and reticence to eat, dampened my mood through the working hours. Am I damaging their instincts? They want so badly to be free.

What a celebration to reenter their outdoor abode on the return home. The enthusiasm rang out across the forest, reminding me that it takes such simple scenes to bring tranquility. As I sat on the homemade stool, I remembered a friend asking me at my last class reunion what I thought I would be doing five years from then. I wondered what his reaction would have been if I had told him I would be sitting in the middle of a birdcage feeling joyously free.

Tuesday

This morning went a little better. After being confined again in the van cage yesterday, Samson and Baby Sister were somewhat more resigned today. Maybe putting in the large flat box filled with dirt and plugs of grass helped, as both seemed a little more contented to have something new to explore. Yet, again, this teaches them to stay on the ground.

Wednesday

I could hear their calls for me as I approached singing "Sup-pa-time," bringing their breakfast. We have become a pretty close group, Samson, Baby Sister, and I. I do all the work; they provide all the entertainment.

A local newspaper heard about us and asked to do a picture story. How could any doting parent refuse? The photographer climbed in the aviary with me. Samson and Baby Sister ignored him and crawled all over me, feeding from my hand, playing in my hair. Like any proud parent, I told tales of formulas and developmental milestones.

Thursday

A cold front barreled through at 4:00 a.m. with bolting thunder and lashing rain. Fretfully, I fought back fear for those baby birds out there in that big wet world. I reminded myself their little house is sturdy and is more shelter than the other small creatures have, covered only by layers of limbs and leaves. As the winds lightened and the rains diminished, I drifted in and out of sleep, seeing in the movie of my mind two frightened tiny beings experiencing their first test of maturity.

The earth is cleansed this morning and everything glistens. There are large bright but clearing clouds overhead and alternating moments of light misty rain. Now it is I who feels the curiosity. What will I find, I ponder, while breathing out "Sup-pa-time," as I approach the outdoor nursery.

Two babies came to me, hungry and responsive to my whispered calls, our moods matching in a kind of suppressed intense arousal, our senses sharpened by the crispness of the earth. Samson and Baby Sister gulped some gruel and caught a cricket or two but quickly rejoined each other on their favorite perch up under the miniature roof. There they stayed, fluffy and cute, looking past me, their eyes never wider, wondering what had happened to their world. Moments of soft rain sounds dabbling on the tar paper covering captured and kept their attention. Sounds in the forest seemed more crystal clear in the clean air and Samson and Baby Sister stretched in unison to absorb their meanings. What lessons do Mother Nature's storms teach her little earth creatures? Is it her way of sharpening sensitivity to different forms of danger?

By mid-morning the rain moved east and Samson's and Baby Sister's interest returned to the twig toys and frayed string of the aviary.

DAY THIRTY-THREE

Friday

I am glad I scheduled this, another Friday, out of the office, so this, with two more, will allow three days in the larger bird house without interruption. Samson and Baby Sister need all the survival training I can give them. My duty is to enjoy them in all ways that prepare them to be free. Yet, I cannot imagine the day they will be gone. In my mind, Samson and Baby Sister will build nests on my land and have babies and their babies will have babies and their babies will have babies and on and on forever. How delightful! I will be a grandparent and a great-grandparent and a great-great-grandparent. I believe it is these kinds of daydreams that nourish the soul and are vitamins for our minds.

With Baby Sister playing on my shoulder, I fed Samson on my hand while telling them of my dream. Samson showed his approval by playing games with me, holding onto the toothpick more tightly than usual and not swallowing his food, all the while fluttering his wings at me and gurgling silly sounds. He seems to know I have to get a respectable grip on the toothpick to keep his little broken beak from looping around the wood so tightly that he pulls it from my hand. (I used to grip the thermometer between my teeth when my mother tried to pull it out of my mouth. I wonder if Samson thinks his behavior is as cute as I thought mine was.)

In the soft spring afternoon, a friend brought a bowl full of those little sow bugs that roll up when touched. Samson and Baby Sister took to them like a child to chocolate candy. To keep the bugs from crawling away, I filled a large shallow pan loosely with dirt, moistened it with water, and poured all the roly-polies across the bottom.

Baby Sister immediately hopped into the pan and struck up a squealing dance that should have won her a silver trophy, causing Samson and me to look at each other in humorous disbelief. Samson grasped the edge of the pan and tilted his body in for a bug or two, but for the longest time, he studied his little sister as if she had gone cuckoo.

I asked the roly-poly bug supplier to bring more and to spread the word. Many people are wanting to see Samson and Baby Sister, but regretfully I discourage this because of apprehension my babies will not fear humans adequately. At this point, cats and humans and the omnivorous crow are my greatest fears. Once Samson and Baby Sister are free, should they attempt to light on another human being, I imagine a person's natural response would be to shoo them away.

A beautiful little bird tries to land on someone's shoulder to say hello and the person harshly swats it away. What a cruel way to teach how dangerous the human being can be. I suppose it is through similar experiences that human babies learn similar dangers.

My mom always asked me to offer a solution along with problems I posed. Of course, she wanted a practical solution. Nevertheless, in the tranquil atmosphere of my babies' home, my mind ebbing to and fro on an imaginary tide, the solution I shared with Samson and Baby Sister was to make every creature ever born able to speak a common language. That way I could teach Samson and Baby Sister to ask for permission before landing on another human being. At least for the moment, this make-believe solution seemed to ease my apprehensions.

DAY THIRTY-FOUR

Saturday

A new plant saucer water bowl was positioned toward the north end of the aviary first thing this morning. Baby Sister in her usual loving way greeted me, inspected me, and talked to me before turning her interest elsewhere. Part of her routine is to play on my shoulders and pull my hair until I laugh. Then she seems satisfied, from there moving into games with Samson, especially playing hide-and-seek around the cricket box. In the middle of the activities, she is prone to come and lean in to me,

"I did not know baby birds play like puppies and kittens. Where one was the other wanted."

holding breathlessly still, so tiny and warm.

Sometimes children in my office do this. It is something unspoken and special. These little children and Baby Sister make up the tender side of the world.

Samson usually is more preoccupied with whatever I have in my hands. He welcomes me playfully, but is quick to investigate. Some children in my office are like Samson, insisting on questioning and investigating everything in view. What wondrous questions they can ask. What persistence Samson can display, checking out camera buttons and openings from every vantage point. These little children and Samson make up the adventurous side of the world.

Yet, this morning Baby Sister was a little out of character. No sooner had I set the new water bowl on the ground and balanced myself on the homemade stool than she dropped onto the edge of the bowl. She took a sip, stuck her beak in the water quite abruptly, then shook the excess water from her nose. Slowly at first she ducked her head deeper into the water, each time followed by greater amounts of shaking. After several dipping episodes, she fluttered vigorously as if wet all over. This told me Baby Sister was close to taking her first bath.

The roly-poly bug friend (I kept the expression to myself) returned in early afternoon with more of the little "chocolate" morsels. From outside the aviary, she quietly observed Samson's and Baby Sister's antics, both awed and amused.

Without warning, Baby Sister went to the water bowl and repeated her head dunking. Suddenly, she hopped squarely into the middle of the bowl and sat down, seemingly holding her breath for a moment like a kid anticipating an icy pool. Then the shaking began.

She had discovered "strawberry shortcake," wanting more and more. She played and splashed and played and splashed. It was the longest baby bird bath in history, with most of the liquid finding its way onto the ground. She had waited for an audience so she could show off, it seemed. (I remember waiting until one of my mama's friends dropped by to visit before I decided to practice my piano recital piece for the hundredth time.) Samson watched from overhead, tolerating his little sister's recital. This was the first major developmental milestone in which Baby Sister preceded Samson.

DAYS THIRTY-FIVE THROUGH FORTY

Sunday

Mother's Day. If only all mothers of the world could feel as fulfilled as I. One of the "chocolate" bug supplier friends came to visit in the early afternoon and brought her mother and aunt to see my baby birds as a treat for Mother's Day. Samson and Baby Sister responded very warmly to the friendly greetings, coming to the wire and pecking at friendly fingers.

Although wanting to share Samson and Baby Sister, repeatedly I question if other fingers will be as friendly. It is of interest to me to see how my birdies behave in these situations. It is also of interest to me to see how other human beings respond to Samson and Baby Sister. The ooh's and ah's and expressions of delighted disbelief were more enthusiastic than I anticipated. Perhaps I have underestimated how incredible others also may feel my bluebirds are.

So much of Samson's and Baby Sister's behavior has come as a surprise to me. I did not know baby birds play like puppies and kittens. A little homemade shelf suspended by nylon string looped through the wire has become one of Samson's and Baby Sister's most prized playgrounds. With the cricket box on one end of the shelf and the food cup on the other, a natural pathway exists, leaving just enough room to play hide-and-seek.

For a half hour at a time, Samson and Baby Sister chase each other, alternately pecking at each other's feet and tail feathers. Such contented kids I never have seen. Their play inspired me to pursue more props. Mulberry branches loaded with ripe fruit were fastened here and there to the aviary walls. Samson was on inspection patrol even before the branches could be anchored.

In these few afternoon hours, both baby birdies have become remarkably agile in landing and balancing on small unstable branches. Surely this is good practice for the nearing date of freedom.

Monday

At home, each time my dad rounded my end of the dining room table to approach his chair, it was routine for him to pat me on top of the head and ask me how my head got so flat. I would tell him in equal good humor it was from his patting me on the top of my head, from whence I got the nickname, "Baby Flattop." I always felt a little as if I was on top of the fun on the rare occasions when I showed up in curlers and he could not get to my head. Then the routine would change slightly, Dad saying teasingly, "Do you know how strange a Baby Flattop looks with 'culverts' in her hair?" Today, I received the supreme confirmation.

I washed my hair early and before rolling it, I took food and fresh water to the aviary, the common procedure for Samson, Baby Sister, and me. They are satisfied to play in my hair whether damp or dry. And again as usual, they landed on the top of my head, then ran back and forth on my shoulder and pulled vigorously in every direction on my stringy hair. An hour later, I returned as I never had done before with my hair rolled in "culverts." Samson went wild, circling my head repeatedly squealing his disapproval and refusing to land. Baby Sister retreated to the lowest and farthest perch and looked up at me crying for food, but refusing to approach. Perhaps even the smallest of God's creatures will tell us something about ourselves if we are willing to listen.

Tuesday

Just as I was about to leave my office this afternoon, a woman in one of the therapy groups who has been a part of all the bluebird episodes burst in the door. She spoke my name in a way I never had heard before and I knew something had healed in her heart. The new grin on her face and the change in her attitude brought her the kind of beauty that exists only in the presence of a smile.

"Samson!" she said.

"Baby Sister!" she said.

"What!" I said.

"Those two baby bluebirds have flown around in my head until I couldn't stand it any more, nagging, nagging, nagging at me to open the door and I did, I did, I did!" and she burst out into laughing tears.

She understood.

Finally, she understood the risk of bondage from not getting involved.

A victim of her father's molestations as a child, she had married a young farmer whose brutality to her and their young daughter had caused her to build a shell from life's miseries. Instead of confronting her husband, she cowered in fear—just as she had with her father.

But now, for nearly two hours, she poured out her understanding of how two baby bluebirds, born out of tragedy, had provided the meaningful prodding necessary to lead her out of her self-imposed imprisonment and into the light.

"As long as there are bluebirds . . . " I started to say.

" . . . there will be miracles and a way to find happiness," she finished.

Wednesday

By this time in the wilds, Samson and Baby Sister would be familiar with all of my land, exploring with their brothers and sisters, guided by their natural parents. In three days, their explorations will begin, and with no guidance from me.

Ridiculous images of me running with a ladder from tree to tree with baby food in hand keep fluttering across my mind. I wonder if Baby Sister's naps against my stomach and on my collar are nearing an end. I wonder if Samson's playful inspections of me are numbered. It is painful to think about that. I know they must be moved from mine to Mother Nature's breast where she and I both know they belong. All this monologue in my mind tells me I am trying to convince myself of something.

Snapshots were returned today, displaying again how much Samson and Baby Sister have changed. Parents forget.

Thursday

Their beauty becomes more visible as their baby coat diminishes and hints of orange show through, especially on Samson's breast. Like the arrival of a baby tooth, there was no orange, and suddenly there is a tiny feather. Their darkening pure sky-blue wings and tail feathers glisten, particularly in the early mornings when the sun's rays are most reflective. I do not know which came first, Samson's way of spreading his wings over his prey just before capture, or the sudden increase in the beauty of his wings. It is of interest to me that these two events coincided. The first time I noticed, I gasped in Baby Sister's ear, "Look at Samson! How beautiful!" I am not just raising baby birds. I am raising the most magnificent creatures on earth. Uh-oh, here I go again.

Friday

All is in readiness for the big flight tomorrow except for Big Mama. I think I can keep my apprehensions to myself and Samson and Baby Sister will never know. Freeing them is what this venture is all about.

A crow the size of a chicken has been in the area all day. Four baby chicks were missing this morning, probably food for a fox. Baby Sister still retrieves bugs too slowly. What do mothers do with their nerves when their children are about to leave home?

The morning's opening brought a light misty rain. If the temperature had been cold, the ground would be blanketed with snow. The morning feeding went as usual, eager, sweet, responsive, full of expression, playful, then sleepy. Twenty-four hours have brought even more flecks of orange on Samson. The shape of their heads looks more and more adult, except when Samson and Baby Sister are nestled together or sleeping. Then they remain babyish looking, fluffy and round.

At noon, I wore an old gray-colored hospital jacket with scroll name written in red above the pocket. Baby Sister took to the writing. She traced the letters over and over with her beak. I found myself sounding out the letters to her, as if teaching a child to spell. I assured myself that part of the fun of this project was noting my own reactions. With Baby Sister learning letters, Samson was examining the buttons on the camera in my hand. I could not move. I did not want to. I could have stayed there forever.

The day ended with a special treat. Samson and Baby Sister simultaneously hopped on opposite sides of the water bowl, simultaneously hopped into the water, and simultaneously began to splash. I had suspected they had practiced this performance for mama early in the afternoon. Always before, the chase was around the cricket box. Now, it was around and around the water bowl. Samson lifted to a perch to groom. Baby Sister hopped to the top of my boot, leaving droplets of water running down my leg to my sock. For a dozen minutes, she groomed herself, her wing tips tickling my leg, then she turned to chew the raveled threads on the leg of my shorts.

All of these times are special, but none is as special as the final moment of nightfall. The last visit of the day is the only time I do not call, "Sup-pa-time." It is a simple little ceremony, saying and cooing good night to each other. While I whispered nose to nose in the quiet spring darkness, I still could feel the dampness on my sock.

DAY FORTY-ONE

Saturday

Graduation day. I was dreaming Baby Sister's little bathed body was dripping water on my cheek, but it was a tear rolling into my ear that awakened me. Now I know

"Samson helped until I hardly could get anything accomplished. He was intrigued by the large wire cutters and the red buttons on my gloves."

a tear rolled into my mama's ear on the days my brother and I left for college.

It had been a restless night. Every hour of light for the past five weeks has revolved around the care of two bluebird babies and today I am going to set them free. This day will tell how their instincts have blended with my training.

Morning duties were dedicated to finishing and installing the freedom window, initially excluded because its measurements and fittings would have delayed assembly of the aviary. I do think adding the window is the thing to do. I do want Samson and Baby Sister to have access to their home should they desire for whatever reason. Children must have a way to return home.

Once the window was in place on the outside, I crawled through the tiny human door to cut out an opening from the inside. Samson helped until I hardly could get anything accomplished. He was intrigued by the large wire cutters and the red button on my gloves. And Baby Sister chose to sit in my hair to watch.

By mid-afternoon, everything was ready: the cameras loaded, the dogs calmed, the day beautiful—and I was about to have a nervous breakdown. I left Samson and Baby Sister a little hungry hoping this would discourage them from wandering too far.

With my hand on the latch, I paused. I do not know why—or maybe I do. Oh so slowly, I lowered the window and stepped back, holding my breath, my heart pounding in my ears. Samson and Baby Sister looked at me quizzically with expressions of curiosity like kids entering a carnival. It was Baby Sister who flew first, straight from her perch to the nearest treetop. Her reaction was one of "Wow-ee," straining her neck to the east, then to the west taking in all she could see. Except for bathing, this was the first time she had preceded big brother in such a giant step. Samson continued to study the situation.

"Come fly, little fellow, reach for the sky," I whispered.

He hopped to the window ledge and paused, looked up and down and at me, up and down and at me. Then he stretched his wings like an eagle and burst into the air, with Baby Sister joining him, soaring around and around and around overhead.

Bursts of joy welled up inside of me, watching my children cross the graduation stage. This is what it is all about. Again and again, they encircled my head, their calls spelling out, "Looky, mama, looky," as my brother and I had done a million or so times to our mama over years and years of skating, of bicycling, or merry-go-round rides. I spun with them until I stumbled. Around and around they went, landing and calling to each other, then launching and looping again. In only minutes, Samson dropped to the ground for a bug and Baby Sister nabbed a worm on a branch.

It was happening. It was really happening. They were flying and seeking food on their own and staying close to my protection. Samson spread his incredibly blue wings over an ant bed to investigate what so many crawly creatures in one place was all about. Baby Sister found another worm on another branch.

Then disaster struck.

Without warning, the female parent of the nesting box in the area darted forth, attacked Samson with a harsh scolding, and ran him far up the hill to a pine grove. In rapid succession, the male struck out at Baby Sister. What had I done? All the books say bluebirds will adopt bluebirds. It never occurred to me that adult bluebirds would be territorial against babies.

A sickening feeling rushed through me. I had taught my babies that home is squarely in the middle of someone else's territory. Out of frustration, Samson and Baby Sister began to snap at each other. I had to resist the impulse to snatch them up and return them to safety. They must learn that the world is not gentle.

The adults attacked several more times over the next two and one-half hours of freedom, but then moved back very quickly, probably because of my presence. Between attacks, Baby Sister did get a lot of food-seeking practice on a tree overhead, chasing ants and bugs over every inch of a three-foot area. And Samson did admirably well in moving from branch to ground, from branch to ground, feeding himself but spending too much time on the ground.

When they attacked, those adult bluebirds seemed to come out of nowhere. Very abruptly, the male drove

Samson against the side of his home not two feet from the freedom window where I was standing. Instinctively, I reached for him and he easily accepted my protection. I drew him back into the safety of his house and closed the window. Baby Sister lit on a low branch and was calling for me even before I could get out of the aviary door. I simply reached out and lifted her to me and carried her back inside. I had worried I would not be able to return them to the aviary, but with ease, I brought them home.

For an instant, both babies spit at each other to keep a distance. As any bewildered parent might do seeing this behavior, I stuffed both with as much food as they would take, hoping this would settle them down. Scarcely before he could swallow, Samson was sound asleep and slept hard for 20 minutes. Baby Sister remained very wide-eyed for a minute or two, overwhelmed with it all, then fell quickly into slumber. Likewise overwhelmed, I dropped onto the homemade stool to absorb all that had just happened.

There had been some funny moments. Neither baby knew how to drop from an overhead branch and slow down to land on me when trying to come for a bite of food. When I stood in the middle of the clearing and called, "Sup-pa-time," each would zoom at me, bypass me, land facing the opposite direction on a branch on the other side of the clearing, turn around, and look down at me as if to say, "Oops, what did I do wrong?" then try it again, winding up back on the same or a nearby branch from where each started.

They did not know how to drop from a distance, then hover, a behavior not required by other babies this age fed by their real parents in the trees. To remedy the predicament, I dug a hole and placed an old branch about the height of my shoulder just outside the freedom window. They learned to fly to the branch and then eat from there, or hop to my hand for food. After numerous trials, they were quite proficient in landing easily wherever they chose and regardless of the height of their drop.

After an hour and an icy lemonade, I returned to discuss the situation with Samson and Baby Sister. They were a little distant with each other as anyone would be after being attacked repeatedly, but their activity and play continued to soften as they pursued their usual adventures about the aviary, seemingly appreciating being protected from those adults feeding energetically outside. All through these past days, as those adults have chirped and gone about their nesting duties, I have wondered if some of their conversation had been directed toward my babies. It tickled me to think the communication might be between true parent and child. Now I feel these are not Samson's and Baby Sister's original parents, as I had thought at first.

The episodes of the afternoon pretty much confirmed my suspicions that the sparrows killed my babies' mother. She simply was absent far too many hours. I believe her death preceded the successful attack on the nesting box.

At bedtime, it was good to see Samson and Baby Sister were buddies again, leaning into each other. They were at peace. Half of me was at peace and half of me was perplexed. I simply do not know what to do. Should I turn these vulnerable beings loose, knowing that those adults will attack again in my absence, driving Samson and Baby Sister away, ill–prepared to survive on their own, putting them in conflict about returning to the only home they know and to mama for food? They would be easy prey if they tried to sleep on high branches without a vigilant parent nearby. All I know to do is give myself a night to ponder the predicament. For now, I feel the relief of seeing Samson and Baby Sister safe and satisfied side by side.

As I sauntered slowly toward the perch of my own home, the title of Maya Angelou's book kept turning in my mind, "I Know Why The Caged Bird Sings."

DAY FORTY-TWO

Sunday

Five-thirty a.m. and I have been in conference with myself half of the night. There had been no choice but to cage Samson and Baby Sister from the very beginning if their lives were to be saved. Yet, how do I determine how much is too much caging and how much vulnerability is in too much freedom? A decision has come to me and I will live with it, right or wrong. There is no doubt now that when, not if, but *when* set free, Samson and Baby Sister will adapt to the wilds. Yesterday told me that.

The dilemma is what condition will they be in if they try to stay close to their home and me and food, and are attacked repeatedly? The adult bluebird assaults probably will be especially vicious when their nestlings fly. If my count is correct, in ten days the parents should have their offspring in the trees and moving toward the forest. That has been the usual pattern of many nestings of many parents in the past. In eight to ten days after that, adult bluebirds typically begin the renesting process.

Once the nesting box is vacated, my intention is to remove all boxes north of my home, set my babies free, then establish new boxes about a mile away. I do not want to drive the adults out altogether; however neither do I want to pit Samson and Baby Sister against well-seasoned, skillfully flying, protective adults intent on defending their chosen territory. I think I can live with this plan.

By 6:00 a.m., I was in the aviary announcing my aims to my little audience. They cooed at my mumblings and ran all over me, on my lap, over my arms, on my head, across my shoulders, under my hair, pecking at my ears, and pulling at my collar like puppies chewing and growling and tugging at a toy.

Included in my scheme will be keeping the birdhouse stocked with new and varied props, making a taste of the outside world more available inside where we will wait for the time to pass. Baby Sister stuffed two mulberries in her mouth when one was more than sufficient. In rapid fire, she threw her neck forward and pop, pop, down each berry went. For the longest time, she sat perfectly still, as though rather regretful. Forgetting about this sizable lunch for such a little girl, shortly afterward I offered her a nibble of home cooking. I told myself it was coincidental, but she lifted a foot at me as if about to scratch her ear, but instead paused in mid-motion. Her appearance was that of a guest refusing third helpings at Thanksgiving dinner. Are all parents amused when they think their kids know what they are doing?

The day drifted lazily on and I was admitting a certain satisfaction with the situation. I just about have myself convinced that a few days' delay will not substantially alter the course to freedom. With Baby Sister perched on my collar, Samson perched on my shoulder, and me perched on the homemade stool, all of us were nearly nodding off when a dead branch came crashing with a thud on the aviary roof. The restraint of trying not to jump almost disjointed my shoulder. Samson and Baby

Sister jumped enough for all three of us. Removing the branch from the roof brought another prop idea . . . a swinging perch. The branch was shortened, holes were drilled through each end and strings were attached.

By nightfall, except for routine worries, I secretly felt well resigned to my decision, even more convinced after observing those adult bluebirds gathering more and more food from the birdhouse grounds. No sooner had I told Samson and Baby Sister about my secret than they struck up a hot pursuit game of flying from the distant end of the aviary to the swinging perch and back again. What a rally it was, reminding me of my brother's and my raucous enthusiasm when told there was to be a picnic at the White Sands National Park close to our home in New Mexico. As quickly as they had charged into their games of chase, Samson and Baby Sister lit in their bedtime corner, signaling me the pillow fight was over. And so, I gathered up my secrets, blew a kiss to my kids, and shuffled toward my home, accepting that I am looking forward to the next two weeks. After all, it is fate that has forced me into making the decision. What else can I do?

DAYS FORTY-THREE THROUGH FORTY-EIGHT

Monday

Arrangements were made with the "chocolate" pill bug supplier to provide afternoon feedings for Samson and Baby Sister this week. No longer will they have to tolerate the confinement of the van cage and be transported back and forth to the city. Now, both babies fare quite well for longer and longer periods of time without supplementary feedings. Now, they study their well-stocked territory intently and chase whatever moves.

The word chase still applies to Baby Sister as she often chases but does not catch. Crickets hide quickly once turned loose and only move occasionally as in the wilds. It does seem to simulate the outside world, and Samson and Baby Sister have to study their turf in order to seek their supper. If not sufficiently satisfied, Samson may beat Baby Sister to the bug and occasionally even take a cricket away from her if she waits too long to gulp it down, which she is prone to do. Sometimes she simply gets a grip on the cricket and then just stands there. Like the infant and the ice cream cone, sometimes the family dog downs the dessert during the delay. I think that with my brother and me, more often I was the "family dog."

If, during a chase, the cricket does not keep moving, Baby Sister continues to have difficulty discriminating between cricket and camouflage even if the critter is squarely under her. Often she looks up at me for approval whether her mouth is full of cricket or a mess of grass, leaves, or dried bark.

It is more and more a habit for both baby bluebirds to spread their azure wings over their prey. Then comes the squeaky warning and the momentary wing fluttering before the attack. When taking food from me, they are more babyish in their squeal and flutter. Although Baby Sister comes to me first, routinely both wind up side by side on my hand. With Samson on my wrist, Baby Sister grips my index finger, and with her nose over the food cup, she helps me with a lifting motion, ducking down and following the end of the toothpick into and out of the cup bottom and into her mouth.

It was lonely in the van today. These were the first

hours away from Samson and Baby Sister in weeks. It appeared they were slightly more in tune to each other and to the forest than to me after spending more time to themselves. The effect is good, I think. Hopefully, in time, with less human contact, they will avoid humans altogether.

After so many hours apart, during the closing thoughts of the day as I studied the activities inside that earthen playhouse, the contrast of being in and out of Samson's and Baby Sister's presence came home even more strongly to me. Perhaps if everyone in the world at the end of his day would find himself a birdhouse, there would be no more wars and no need for tranquilizers.

Tuesday

The sun's reflection on Samson's and Baby Sister's coats early this morning highlighted the incredible beauty that lies under their baby feathers. Every dawn brings a new gift of color surprise, little packages wrapped in deeper blue with soft speckled gray on white and a tiny bow of faint orange across the middle. What proficient little fliers they are becoming. Maybe the variety of props is helping.

Rain in walls of water, then tornado alerts came in late afternoon. I wanted to fly home. Storms are too big and baby birds are too little.

I arrived late from work in a misty quiet rain. Quickly, I changed into shorts and boots, and with flashlight and umbrella, trekked across the back ridge of wet grass to my babies' room, talking softly as I approached. What might a woodsman think should he happen upon this scene of a high-stepping, long-legged creature in boots and shorts with a flashlight in one hand and an umbrella in the other, talking to herself? I believe God, and lovers of little life, and other doting parents would understand.

I pressed my nose to the wet wire and whispered lullaby language to the tiny snuggled babies fast asleep inside, ever, ever so small, and retired to my journal, noting that baby bluebirds talk in their sleep.

Wednesday

Samson and Baby Sister and I dined together this evening. I took my supper of noodles with cheese and salads to the bird house. Baby Sister was courteous enough to sit on my thumb which held my plate and ask for bites, but her mischievous big brother stepped squarely in the potato salad and had himself a strawberry and then a raisin from the fruit salad. Baby Sister took some tastes of an apple slice, but then politely asked to be fed. Arranging a few bites of her homemade food along the edge of the plate kept her happy. I have become admirably more courageous but not enough to stick a half dead cricket in my noodles to pacify a baby bluebird.

I wish I had an automatic camera that would record how much they play when I am away. In my presence, they are continuous comedians—and how they love each other. It is a routine for them to show off for me, playing hide-and-seek around the cricket box, tugging at the strings holding the shelves taut against the wire, doing trapeze acts off the swinging perch, and bounding from branch to branch in games of follow-the-leader, talking to each other sweetly as all the world should do. Every few minutes, one will find a new position and proudly display an attitude of "Home free home! I'm safe, ha-ha, can't get me!"

If one baby gets closer to the end of a perch, the other automatically wants to be there, as my brother and cousin and I did when each of us wanted the outside seat by the car window. The methods Samson and Baby Sister use to get each other to move away from the outside wall are not particularly subtle. If Baby Sister is outside, Samson will move her by sticking his head under her bottom and raising up just enough to sway her off balance. As she scurries to right herself back onto the perch, he steps proudly across the branch to the end, both jabbering back and forth at each other all the while. Then to regain her lost place on the perch, Baby Sister sort of crawls up and sits on Samson's head until he tilts over and, with a giggling attitude, Baby Sister recaptures the end position, scrambling over quickly in the second it takes Samson to right himself.

Why do these baby bluebirds make me feel so philosophical? I suppose it is because their play is so nourishing, the way so much of children's play was when youngsters had to work hard to make their own fun before the electronic age. My brother and I created every game imaginable in our homemade dugout in the vacant lot near our home. We are different because of those games. And my brother is the most gentle man I have ever known. Now two playful baby bluebirds have brought back those warm, wonderful memories in such a special way.

Thursday

The "chocolate" pill bug supplier is leaving me progress notes regarding Samson's and Baby Sister's welfare, just like a regular babysitter.

This is the fourth day of long afternoons alone for Samson and Baby Sister, except for the babysitter's visit. The plan is going well, I think, and my kids seem satisfied and well nourished.

It no longer surprises me how responsive the individuals I work with are to my bluebirds and to the issues of taking risks. A modest middle-aged man burst into group therapy tonight as enthusiastically as the woman broke into my office two weeks ago. He was as full of himself as Samson was when he captured his first cricket.

The fellow took center stage for the evening as he acknowledged how his insecurities had enslaved his wife, his sons, and his daughter. The children had not known fun and flexibility from him. His wife had not known affection and affirmation from him, and the effects inhibited and frightened every fiber of their being as his father's shamings and demands for perfection had intimidated him.

For an hour, he used flying hand gestures to describe huge hamburgers, home runs, horseback rides, hickory tree swings, and a mountain of marshmallows. The family had launched their new lives into freedom with their first picnic.

Together, he pledged in a voice of allegiance, they would learn to fly.

Friday

More flecks of brilliant blue are peeking through on Samson's right shoulder this morning and another tiny orange feather is present on his breast: God's promise to clothe His little creature in nature's finest. Baby Sister's coat is maturing more slowly, with fluffy baby down still covering most of her breast and tummy. She continues to come to me first and linger longer. Samson answers food calls from a longer distance, then hops to my hand and eats. His attention returns to flying insects and nature outside more quickly. This pleases me. His vigilance may protect both of them once freed.

Why do I feel compelled to say good night each evening after work in the dark or moonlight or in the rain or fog? If I could explain what I find, what I see, what I hear, what I carry back into my home, perhaps no explanation would be needed. If it is the child who gets tucked in, what is it that makes the mama feel so good?

I stroked Baby Sister's wings as she cooed to me sleepily. She was on the outside. It told me she probably had sat on Samson's head before bedtime. Sometimes my big brother humored me, too, but I did not have to stand on his head to get my way.

Saturday

"Oh! What a beau-ti-ful morning," I sang while skipping to the birdhouse, tattered straw hat on my head. A day for working in the yard. Samson and Baby Sister did not think my hat was funny, and told me in unmistakable chirpings what to do with it. After all, one of their favorite landing strips is in the middle of my hair. I apologized and laid the hat aside. In only moments, however, that hat began to move. Baby Sister had crawled under the brim, got a grip on one of the straws, and begun her playful tug. Samson quickly joined her and the two of them proceeded to drag that object of straw ten times their weight across the floor.

After three hours on my lawn tractor, I returned to the aviary with a large tumbler of iced tea in hand, this time politely laying my hat just outside the door. Baby Sister landed on one of my fingers and tipped her beak into the glass for a taste. I invited Samson for a sip but he declined.

Years ago, the first months I had a tiny toy poodle, I washed my hands before meals. In a year, she was sitting in my lap during meals. The third year, she licked the edge of my plate. After a while, love is what is most important.

Samson and Baby Sister were playing in my hair when the male bluebird from the nesting box landed on the dead limb I had set up just outside the freedom window. Both babies responded frenetically, flying nervously and crying their displeasure. Shortly afterward, the adult moved on. I appreciated the reminder that my decision to delay was a good one.

During the week, the bird babysitter, in a progress note addressed me as "Big Perch." At bedtime, I told Samson and Baby Sister about it. I swear, for a second they looked each other straight in the eye and chirped, then back at me in unison. I know it was coincidental, but truly I would be tempted to give half of everything I own to know what they said.

DAY FORTY-NINE

Sunday

I have just been nestled and nudged, climbed all over, walked on, and every button and fray pecked and pulled, and every hair on my head tugged on twice. Celebrating just to be alive is the best kind of celebration.

This afternoon at the hardware store, I heard two men loudly bragging about the number of squirrels and doves they had killed on their last hunt. Later, I saw them drive away in their expensive cars. Had they learned to kill—or never learned *not* to kill? Surely they did not need those little animals for food. I wondered if those men ever could be taught to feel the greater exuberance of knowing the love of a playful little squirrel or a dove, ironically named the love bird, than of killing them. A hopeless goal, I suspect.

It is true all the boys I see in my office who needlessly kill animals are angry. Maybe those men have angry boys inside them.

As I sat in the aviary with my babies playing on my shoulders and in my hair, so innocently trusting, I thought of those men's conversations. I felt sick and frightened thinking about all the little creatures being slaughtered. I thought of a squirrel family I have known for ages. One baby climbed down inside the small hole of the feeder hanging at my dining room window and ate as she sat in the sunflower seeds. Her brother hung by his toenails down the side of the oblong feeder and ate upside down, plucking one seed at a time out of a tiny feeder hole. Those two playful siblings came with their parents to my window for weeks and weeks. Two days after squirrel season started last year, only one came.

I worry about Samson and Baby Sister and little boys and BB guns. There is a law against shooting song birds, but the rule is useless to an uninformed youngster with his new Christmas weapon. Why would anyone want to give a child a gun on Christ's birthday? Perhaps it is just one more of mankind's thoughtless deeds and truly is not intended to teach harm. Yet, it does not teach peace, and besides, who is the typical victim of a boy and his BB gun? Perhaps it all is a matter of being innocently unconcerned, the way mankind sees without awareness the devotion of all the little families around him. It is not a matter of simple thoughtlessness, however, when mankind throws pets out on country roadsides. Slow, agonizing deaths usually follow from depression, thirst, and starvation. I believe in the end the death comes from a broken heart.

Blessed are the fathers who teach their sons about the law against killing songbirds. I told Samson and Baby Sister that perhaps someday I would tell their story to the world. If they inspire just one little boy to put down his BB gun, and just one adult to notice the joy of little families all around, my duty would be done.

Suddenly, I realized Samson and Baby Sister were chirping and chattering at me as if in a great debate, passionately involved in conversation. For the thousandth time, I had been expressing all these thoughts aloud and my babies simply were putting in their two cents' worth.

Later this afternoon, a booming rainstorm plowed through. Samson and Baby Sister visibly cowered at the burst of thunder and held more tightly together, unless they were on my shoulder. Otherwise, they now seem to accept a storm simply as one of the mysteries of the earth. After the rain clouds passed and the sky again cleared, fresh mulberry branches were arranged on the birdhouse walls.

The eagerness of both babies to explore never abates. At one point, Samson chose a huge juicy mulberry and

71

began to tug at it. He displayed pride and confidence that he could overpower this sizable prey. In a moment, he popped it into his mouth, made a valiant attempt to swallow it whole, then held still on a branch, looking at me very wide-eyed. Again, he gulped hard, but to no avail. He looked as if he had a ping-pong ball stuck in his throat. Finally, he yielded to defeat, opened his mouth wide, threw his head back and popped the berry out. He studied the berry lying on the ground, then looked up at me with a silly expression on his face. I leaned over, captured that wicked berry, pulled it apart into little seedlets, and Samson ate them one by one out of my maroon-colored hand.

Samson's breast becomes more brilliantly orange each day. Baby Sister's remains white and speckled gray, confirming I have a boy and girl. Still, I wonder how I knew. Fantasies of grandbabies in the spring become more playful in my head.

DAYS FIFTY THROUGH FIFTY-FOUR

Monday

After hours and days of talking to baby bluebirds, one finds oneself undergoing a kind of transformation. It does seem wise occasionally to stop to check what one is becoming. Somehow I feel an inner peace increasingly pervading my mood as my mind blends with nature by way of conversations with Samson and Baby Sister. I am convinced I can talk to baby bluebirds and I am convinced they understand every word. At least, I am convinced we understand a great deal about each other.

Again, there is a light, foggy rain this night and, with my flashlight, shower cap, boots, and red shorty pajamas, I made my way to the birdhouse, slowing and stepping more gently as I neared Samson and Baby Sister. Around the south corner and along the wall with the larger wire to their usual sleeping perch, I began to talk to my fluffy toyish babies. With my tape recorder in hand, I told them good night and they responded ever so quietly in sweet coos. Their whispers can be heard on tape in answer to my voice.

It is reassuring to hear the tape. Perhaps I am not so crazy after all.

Tuesday

Morning feedings and family visits have become such a routine part of my day with Samson and Baby Sister, I wonder what I will do when they are gone. Each day brings something delightfully different, a new feather, a new color, a new action.

A new game started this morning. My crossed arms formed a natural bridge from one side of my body to the other. Whoever gets closest to my elbow, while playing on my forearm, has greater access to both the tattered pockets and the frayed threads on the short sleeve of my faded denim shirt. Where one baby is, the other wants to be; what one chews, the other gnaws; what one pushes, the other pulls.

In the midst of their giddy game, a hush flowed across the forest like the moment before sundown. Samson and Baby Sister paused in unison, cuddled against each other, and warmly leaned into my side. From there, they peered out at the world as they so often are prone to do, listening

73

to the quiet. How long we drifted is immeasurable. It was the "Hey, mama" of the baby titmouse that interrupted the silence.

(Certainly, I will not let Samson and Baby Sister hear me say this but surely the baby titmouse is the cutest of all nestlings. They are tiny, wide-eyed, and have a top knot that stands straight up when they squeal for food. I have recorded them several times to prove their calls sound like "Hey, mama, hey, mama," and with six of them squawking at once, they resemble a nursery of hungry toddlers.)

While leaning into my stomach, Samson and Baby Sister cooed to the baby titmice as one child will to another regardless of race or color.

Wednesday

The day of freedom approaches and again my anxieties are stirring. The same thoughts regarding risks written six weeks ago keep flashing before my mind: to get involved has risks, not to get involved has risks, to do nothing has risks. Each must choose his own brand of risks.

Forty-seven days ago, no attempt needed to be invested in saving these baby bluebirds. They could have been left to die, risking all the joy that has followed. One hundred days ago, all the bluebird nesting boxes could have been left in the barn, avoiding any chance of hurt that came with the sparrows' attack. Five thousand days ago, these ten acres could have been left barren. Repeating these thoughts aloud seems to dispel some of my fears of risks I know will accompany the approaching flight. Of one thing I am certain: caging a bluebird for life is the greatest risk of all.

Sunrise was all pink and blue, colors just made for a baby girl and boy. Baby Sister snuggled up under my collar in the hollow of my neck. I could feel her softly breathing, and hear her heart, so little and yet so big. If something should happen to this baby girl and Samson, I will remember these times and not be sorry. Undoubtedly I will cry, but I will not be sorry.

What a paradox it is that so much danger accompanies freedom. To be free should be the time of greatest safety. Maybe there are no "shoulds."

Thursday

Tomorrow was to be the day to begin freeing Samson and Baby Sister. Yet, when I left for work this morning, the babies in the closest nesting box still had not flown. They were peering out, however, ready to set sail, but this means they still will be in the area. The adult bluebirds are scurrying nervously about all over the place. Saturday will have to be freedom day.

Friday

How about that! Samson and Baby Sister and I are famous. They got their picture in the newspaper today, sitting on some redheaded lady named Big Bird in the caption. Sweet story and a special little picture above the headlines on the front page. I told Samson and Baby Sister about it. They sat in my hair.

The trees close by are full of baby bluebirds from the nesting box. And the parents strongly warn me to stay back, diving at my head in threatening determination to keep their offspring protected as I enter the aviary. At another time, I would have monitored and filmed every movement those cute little fledglings made. They remind me of Samson and Baby Sister at that age.

Naturally, Samson and Baby Sister were cuter. Next, I will be carrying pictures in my purse and bragging about them to strangers.

DAY FIFTY-FIVE

Saturday

Five a.m. and out across the grassy ridge to the birdhouse I hopped, skipped, and jumped, calling "Sup-pa-time!", dancing a bit like a fool, trying to ease my apprehensions and express my feelings of celebration at the same time. The snappy air made me bouyant and the sunrise, unequaled in its beauty, made me happy. Samson and Baby Sister acted as giddy as I.

All the preparations of the initial flight were readied by 10:00 a.m. However, the adult bluebirds could be seen about 200 yards down the power line to the northeast. Periodically, they would fly toward the barn and drop for food, carrying it back to their family in some distant pine tree.

Again, I whispered parental warnings from outside the aviary and lowered the freedom window an inch at a time. The babies inside were so involved with their own recreation they showed no concern for the world outside the wire.

I called Samson to come join me. He dropped to the floor of his house and beat up a dead leaf. I called again and, as if without a care in the world, Baby Sister began to stretch her wings and groom herself. I felt like a parent telling her children for the third time to go clean up their rooms.

After several more calls, I crawled inside and tenderly took Baby Sister in my hands, kissed her on top of her velvety head, and opened my hands to the heavens. She paused a moment on my finger tips, then again sailed to the same tree top and peered across the earth, first north then south. She stood so proud, with her head stretched and her breast high. Samson saw this and hopped to the window ledge beside me and, as before, studied the sky, the earth, and me. Softly I reassured him and he lifted gently into the air up and over his home like a toy helicopter and onto a nearby branch. In a flash, both babies united to repeat their first frolicsome flights, zooming into the air and soaring in circles overhead.

All went well until the adult attacks began. These assaults were shorter lived and less vigorous, however, as the parents now have double duty, both to feed their brood and to protect them in the trees. In quick order, they get mulberries, first for themselves, then for their young, and fly off into the distance.

Between spells of playing in the air, Samson and Baby Sister hop about above on branches as they do in their home, and cuddle and converse in coos, play hide-and-seek, and chase each other's tail and toes. It is good to see they are not confused and frustrated this time and, instead of spitting at each other, they are even more attentive to one another in their fun. Perhaps it is their increasing maturity that brings these rewards.

After a couple of hours, however, they tired of those adults' scoldings and moved toward the west several yards behind the mulberry tree into a huge old oak tree. It always has reminded me of a protective grandfather with awesome 75-year-old arms outstretched. Maybe Samson and Baby Sister think so too. At the foot of this massive tree Samson's and Baby Sister's siblings are buried.

For the most part, the adult bluebirds want unlimited access to the mulberry tree located between the birdhouse and the big oak. Therefore, they tend to fill their mouths and move on.

At one point, however, they flew toward the front of my home and along with other birds of the area, nervously screeched at something on the porch. They could be seen hovering for a lengthy period of time over the edge of the steps. Finally, all calmed and the bluebirds flew to join their young toward the north. What was that all about?

Samson and Baby Sister came to me several times for tidbits of food or just to say hello, lighting on my shoulder or hand, then returning to the old grandfather oak. They did very well dropping to the ground for food. A water-filled pot plant saucer was placed on a tree stump nearby. Baby birds could not be seen for the water splashing; fluttering in circles they went like wound-up toy boats in a tub.

After their eight and one-half hours of freedom, and with the light blending into night, I strolled over to the camera sitting high on the tripod and simply asked if they had had enough. Even a bit to my amazement, Samson instantly dropped onto the camera. I gathered him up, and, willingly, he went into the aviary where he waited for Baby Sister to follow. Immediately, she glided down and accepted my hands enclosing her body. She took her place beside her big brother, eagerly chirping to him about their day. Once back in their home, they fluttered about, cooing contentedly, happy to be back on familiar ground.

An hour later, I sat over a cup of tea at my dining room table, reflecting on the fullness of the day, my mind drifting aimlessly. The center window curtain in the sunken living room began to move. A slithery black object showed itself and paused suspended from the middle window ledge. Its shape let me know I had a snake to remove from my living room.

As we stared at each other, the air around my face thickened with fear. So that is what all the commotion was about over the front steps! A few month ago, a new redwood deck was installed on the front porch which changed the height of the floor, leaving a sizable gap between the deck and the bottom of the screen door. Evidently, the snake had crawled under the screen door and made himself at home in my living room and waited for a quiet time to give me a heart attack.

With gloves and hoe and big wastebasket and a screen cover, I captured the big wiggly creature and took it two hundred yards down the drive and across the road, rolled the whole mess into the ditch, and ran as if I had freed a dragon. At dawn the next day, hopefully no one saw me gather up the hoe and basket and screen from the ditch.

Will Samson and Baby Sister appreciate the danger inherent in all this? A snake can find its way into any crack or crevice and into any tree. Samson and Baby Sister surely will have some respect for a "worm" that size.

Yet I cannot keep from worrying. Perhaps there are those who would rebuff me for expressing such an opinion, but at times, I feel that if something should happen to one baby, it would be kinder if tragedy befell them both. One without the other would be inconsolable.

Sunday

Before coffee, baby greetings, or sunrise this morning, I repaired that screen door.

A friend from New Mexico stopped by early for a short visit with camera in hand. Baby Sister immediately took to his hair. Just like a woman.

Later in the morning, I opened the freedom window and called my children. They hesitated again, continuing as usual to frolic about in their big screened playhouse. I crawled into their home and sat for a while on the home-made stool.

Like a three-year-old after devouring a strawberry snow cone, Samson had fresh mulberry juice all down his front. When he was a tiny boy in the nest and did not know how to clean his beak, I would wipe the corners of his mouth where his little crooked beak collected crusty cereal. Now he was a big boy and would wear the mulberry juice for a while, then bathe and groom himself.

As I entered their home, both birdies just looked at me like "Oh boy! Playtime!" unconcerned with the opened window. I acknowledged to them that sitting on me and dancing around the cricket box might be a lot more fun than grubbing for food in the real world, but it was time for aviation practice.

They continued to dillydally, and so I gathered up Samson in my right hand and Baby Sister in my left and cautioned, "Don't go too close to the dogs and don't go too far away and be sure to duck when the adult bluebirds attack and don't stay on the ground too long and if you don't mind, you won't get your mulberry allowance." Dissatisfied with such a series of parental "don'ts," I added, "And do have a good time."

Slowly, I stretched my arms toward the sky and

opened my hands, full of everything meaningful in this life. Samson and Baby Sister lifted in harmony toward the heavens.

Chairs were positioned under the grandfather oak tree, and there the entertainment began, surpassing any day at Disneyland or evening at the theater. Excitement spread all over Samson and Baby Sister when they discovered the television antenna, reaching out like a fish skeleton high above the third floor crow's nest of my home.

It all started when Baby Sister chased a slow fluttering insect up and down, over and around a limb on the old oak. Like little magnets, the bug and Baby Sister zigzagged from the branch to the ground by the water bowl, over to the cross tie retaining wall, across the parking area, up onto the platform of the miniature windmill, horizontally to the sun deck above the carport, and then straight up to the third floor roof top. There rising above her stood the giant jungle gym antenna, begging her to play.

Samson tolerated the distance between Baby Sister and himself for only an instant. Then, zoom, away he went to join her. All aerial ribs were surveyed for bugs, then pecked clean again. They remained aloft for over an hour. My arms ached from holding the binoculars so long, and they left strange looking pressure marks over my eyebrows.

This is the season for tornados. They crawl insidiously across the earth, stalking and ravaging the land like a lion after its prey, leaving deep gashes in the soil, then creep away to the east to feast on the next community. Exclusive of these short-lived violent storms, this spring has been unusually pleasant, with mornings like mountain evenings, and afternoons bringing the light warmth and sweet breezes of a tropical isle. Today was such a day.

81

What more could anyone want for the Memorial Day weekend, soft blue skies and baby bluebirds.

At dusk I called Samson and Baby Sister, and they fluttered down to me like leaves finding rest upon Mother Earth.

With my young ones perched on the tiny bar of the baby cage, I strolled to the birdhouse, tranquil and confident that these youngsters now could fend for themselves and be left to their own devices, if they only knew more about danger.

My speed-demon, fun-loving, rowdy dogs definitely are a major concern. I love my Candi and my Duet.

Duet has a pair of different colored eyes, and Candi has the sweetest disposition imaginable. They stand on their back legs and, with front paws on each other's neck, dance in circles until one tumbles over, then start the entire ballet over again.

Before Duet moseyed up the drive from nowhere several years ago, coughing and close to death from heart worms, Candi was alone much of the time and already had created games for her own entertainment. After dinner each night, she still stages a show across the grassy ridge, throwing her rubber toy dragon high into the air with a toss of her head, then running on her back legs to catch the dragon with her mouth and front feet. The first time I witnessed this, an ice cream cone melted halfway down my arm and a little puppy was catching the droplets by the time I realized what was happening.

And my Duet, she is my shadow, always one step behind my left leg.

They are affable hounds, but they are unpredictable. One of their favorite pastimes is to stop dead still, gaze into each other's face, then bolt simultaneously like dogs out of a race track gate either toward the front of the house to chase squirrels and birds, or toward the north to scatter rabbits and chickens. They do this repeatedly and the fun is in the chase.

But, on very rare occasions, Candi or Duet will catch a baby chicken or rabbit. No amount of scolding has removed the hunting instinct completely. Last week there was an incident. A baby chicken had to be removed from Candi's mouth. It survived uninjured after a period of shock, but such an experience would mean certain death to a baby bluebird. Dare Samson and Baby Sister be left free and unchaperoned?

Not wanting to disturb the spell of the day's successes, in true Scarlett O'Hara style, I put the thoughts of danger aside and promised to make the critcal decision tomorrow, Memorial Day. Now I would put my baby bluebirds to bed and count my blessings.

DAY FIFTY-SEVEN

Monday

I knew this might be my last morning greeting Samson and Baby Sister in their little house, close in together, protected from the world. I knew in a while the freedom window would be lowered, releasing my two little native Americans to their free-flying futures, perhaps never again to know confinement. Today would determine whether to bring them back inside one last night or leave them free forever. I needed time this morning to be with them in their home, to reflect on all our quiet hideaway had beheld.

I climbed in and they climbed on. Maybe they sensed

the need in me because this was the grand finale of play. Several times I chuckled out loud, which just egged them on. It was as if they had it planned, "When Mama comes through the door, let's get her!" I was the plains of Texas, roamed all over by two little buffaloes. I was the stage at the Metropolitan, danced on from apron to backdrop. I was the Smithsonian Institution, every object inspected, nudged and rubbed. I was the Sahara Desert, every grain of sand arranged and rearranged. I was the toy store, every button buzzed, every knob pushed and turned. I was loved.

With a tummy full of crickets and mulberries, Baby Sister one last time crawled down under my collar and nestled as she had in her own baby bed next to Samson day after day during those early times in my home. This is the most affectionate tiny being I have ever known. Samson sat beside her on my shoulder. There we stayed, we three, huddled on the edge of the forest on the side of the earth in our secret place. This was more life as God intended it in this soft sun-sprinkled, star-dusted, screened sanctuary than in all the world's great halls and embassies. The mood summarized all this venture had meant. Never had I been richer.

But I knew it was time to unlock the gate to freedom. Samson and Baby Sister came to me on the window ledge and waited, cooing to me and hesitating, as if still in the mood that had just preceded, as was I. I thanked them and thanked them and thanked them and they lifted my heart with them into the sky.

Friends came to spend the afternoon simply to pass the holiday smiling at Samson and Baby Sister. Like any true parent, I took pride in how well they performed, funny, playful, loving. Each of us found a niche under the grandfather oak and, on limbs reaching to eternity,

Samson and Baby Sister staged the show of the season, between and beside, up and over, around and under they went. Everything that moved was evaluated for lunch, from huge six-inch worms to beetles the size of quarters. Baby Sister became enchanted with a chameleon with his throat ballooned out in crimson red. She chased it 15 feet, three inches at a time, down a branch until it had enough of her peckings at its tail, and finally dropped into a sticker bush below.

Both babies repeatedly spent too much time on the ground, fearless and preoccupied with whatever captured their interest. This is not good. The dogs were moved to greater distances several times for training purposes, but it will not always be possible to take this precaution.

Today's territory expanded to a grove of smaller oak trees off the drive in front of my house. Samson and Baby Sister seem to respect a diamond-shaped boundary marked by these oaks, the grandfather oak, and my house. In my mental wanderings, this area takes the form of a demilitarized zone, where my baby bluebirds happily will stay forever and no enemy can enter.

Samson landed on the vapor light not 18 inches from a male redbird chirping loudly on top of the power pole holding the light. The cardinal crouched low and drew back his top knot and, in his threatening attitude, warned Samson to move back. Samson ducked slightly, but for the most part, stood there, staring at the red-feathered creature.

For a chilling instant, a shiver shot through me. Neither baby bird would know danger until after an attack, as with the adult bluebirds. Baby Sister eagerly would greet any predator with a gleeful invitation to play.

This thought no more began to tantalize my mind than I spotted a tarantula prancing across the ridge in the distance toward the area where Candi and Duet lazily slept in the sunshine. No doubt the prissy little lady would have marched herself right by Candi's and Duet's noses without incident. Yet, I watched Baby Sister's interest mount as she stretched her neck higher and higher, eyeing the spider. I was convinced that in only moments she would be off in friendly pursuit. Had she approached the tarantula at that point, it would have thrown her only inches away from my unpredictable hounds. I do not believe a tarantula is an enemy of a bluebird, but Baby Sister would try to befriend anything that crawled, momentarily leaving her devoid of her already limited vigilance.

Instinctively, I went for the carport and kitchen brooms and with one placed before the fuzzy little creature, I encouraged her to crawl up on it by nudging her gently from behind with the other broom. I must admit she was rather cute. On back feet, she lifted her front legs high into the air and then attacked the straw in a soft, tapping fashion with her front feet functioning as if trying to control an alligator by nudging it in the nose with feathers. Repeatedly she struck at the broom acting as if lightly playing piano chords, then drawing her fingers back into the air, ready for the next chord. Once gathered up on the broom, she rode to the edge of the forest in this regal pose with her body and back legs low and front legs high, reminding me of a princess waving to her crowds.

In coping with these little-creature predicaments, it does seem to help to try to see the situation from the little being's point of view.

Late in the evening, I abandoned any consideration of making this the first night of freedom when ominous clouds abruptly appeared from the west, covering the sun.

Winds rushed at the big oak where my babies were playing, running Samson off to the vapor light pole and Baby Sister to the top of a very tall, leggy tree where she could be seen clutching a limb whipping sharply back and forth against the sky.

I ran for the baby cage and called to my young ones. Initially, they held nervously to their positions, but momentarily, each yielded, dropping into Mama's arms, first Baby Sister, then Samson with a straight dive from the top of the pole as fast as his little body would fall.

I ran ostrich-legged for the birdhouse. For several minutes, blasts of wind swallowed up the warm afternoon air, threatening to gulp up trees and earth as well. As quickly as the storm arrived, it faded into the darkening east, leaving a carpet of coolness behind it. Samson and Baby Sister bathed together and so well enough was left alone.

The day has gone well. The three days of independence training have gone well. An additional night's protection under Mama's wing surely will not alter their journey into freedom.

DAY FIFTY-EIGHT

Tuesday

Dawn was spectacular.

As I met Samson and Baby Sister, they seemed to be revving up their engines in unison with the changing colors, gliding back and forth in synchrony like miniature figurines on a music box, perhaps now more ready to be released to the trees. Their appetites were equally active and their little fuzzy coos asked me for breakfast faster than I could provide it. Baby Sister hovered over my hand until I held still and her raucous big brother zoomed onto my shoulder and literally squawked straight into my ear like a cheerleader into a megaphone. I chuckled so hard food shook off the toothpick.

This, a work day, allowed for limited lingering with my babies, and so, I told them I loved them and opened the freedom window. From attending to my every movement, this time their interests turned more naturally to the outside. Together they hopped to the window ledge and hesitated, reminding me of children waiting for the school bus. Their deepening blue wings shone in radiant iridescence. On the same breath, my little twin rockets shot into the air, launched from this special window, possibly for the last time. For the second it takes a wing to flutter, tears threatened to stream forth, telling me my children might never return home. But the day is serene. There is no reason to hold them from Mother Nature's arms any longer.

After final preparations for work, I fed Samson and Baby Sister under the grandfather oak where I found them playing nonchalantly and chasing bugs.

At last I drove away, leaving them only with the protection of each other. I saw little blue wings in my rearview mirror as I turned down the drive and away from the grandfather oak that was holding my babies' precious lives in its keeping. The thoughts of risks turned over and over in my mind in rhythm with the motor . . . to get involved has risks, to get involved has risks . . . NOT to get involved has risks.

In the misery of the following few hours, worry gnashed at my nerves and my jaw grew sore from teeth grinding. The knowledge that friends were to visit Samson and Baby Sister later in the day would not still my soul.

When an unexpected break came in early afternoon, I ran for my car and flew home. The vehicle still was in motion as I galloped toward the aviary to get the baby food, screeching like a banshee, "Sup-pa-time!," scattering half the wildlife in the forest. But Baby Sister remained undaunted. There she was, hovering over my head, as if telling me, "Hold still, Mama, hold still, so I can land." Evidently, she had accompanied me the length of my race. Immediately, Samson joined us. The deafening swoosh of blood flowing back into my head made me feel top heavy. The only disadvantage to loving baby bluebirds is they cannot be picked up and squeezed.

This was the test, and my babies were beside me. I fed them as air refilled my lungs and my ears cleared.

I completed the remainder of the day and evening at work, no longer feeling on the verge of collapse.

Two hours before midnight, the moon-shadowed ground marking my way, I moseyed across the dewy grass sending lullaby messages into the trees where my babies surely were sleeping. I imagined little arbor elves standing guard, they and not I knowing where Samson and Baby Sister nestled in slumber.

I wondered whether my babies heard my hummings, or if they dreamt of their first day's freedom. I wished them not to be homesick as I was my first night away from home alone in the dorm.

I gasped when a ray from my flashlight caught the movement of a night-crawling predator soundlessly stepping off a branch squarely in the middle of the mulberry tree. I felt an urge to plead aloud to the elves and grandfather oak to do something, but the creature slipped away and into the woods.

And so, I reminded myself that the night with half moon overhead is silent and cool, the kind that cradles all little things in nourishing sleep.

Every door and window in my home was opened to the night, inviting in the moon-shadowed dark air, creating a greater closeness to my babies who in my mind cuddled safely together on a branch.

DAY FIFTY-NINE

Wednesday

Someone said, "I hear bluebirds." It was I, awakening and responding to the sounds. My jump out of bed was so abrupt I knocked over a little TV and caught it in mid-air. Out onto the sun deck I stumbled, determined to find Samson and Baby Sister on the antenna. But no, it was those adult bluebirds keeping herd on their wandering offspring.

The heavens to the west reflected the fiery reds of hell. The burning effect seemed to chase a satellite away to join the bright morning star in the east. I paused a moment, awed by the scene, then spun and bounced down the stairs to warm baby food.

In shorts and flannel shirt, I moved out into the flaming dawn in search of my young ones. I whispered, "Suppa-time," up into every tree, wanting to hear Samson and Baby Sister answer me eagerly, as they always have. It was early but I needed to know they were safe. For 45 minutes, I stood by their little home, watching and listening to nature awakening, resolute that sunrise would bring my children to me.

At 6:00 a.m., Samson appeared without a sound and lit on the feeding branch next to my arm. He responded with light wing flutters but no sound and took little food. I wanted to pick him up and nestle him and kiss him and feel his clean, soft, downy feathers on my cheek. All I could do was tell him at that moment he was the most magnificent creature in the entire world.

For an instant, I thought I heard a coo from the tree above the aviary. It is early; Baby Sister still may be sleeping. From Samson's direction of arrival, perhaps he spent the night over his home, or maybe I needed to believe that to convince myself Baby Sister was nearby.

I studied every inch of the trees. Every speckled piece of bark appeared to be Baby Sister's tiny breast, every leaf her little head, every hint of sound her babyish coo, every movement the flutter of her pastel blue wings.

But no Baby Sister.

Samson lifted off to a familiar tree. A bird landed nearby. Baby Sister! Then I realized the difference. It was a titmouse.

I found myself standing before the freedom window feeding station, just staring. Samson must have sensed my worry. He dropped onto the artificial branch by my arm and there he stayed, motionless. We stared at each other. He looked bewildered, so wide-eyed and so silent.

When he returned to the nearby tree, I hurried for the lounge chair and as soon as I sat down Samson came to join me. Sitting on the low end by my feet, he looked up at me ever so long, trying to tell me something I refused to know. His velvety orange fluffy feathers fluttered in the soft morning breeze, reminding me in the midst of my worry of his increasing beauty. There he remained, seemingly needing to be close to mama.

Again, he moved to the closest branch. A titmouse

baby crying for food appeared, squealing loudly just before his parent quieted him with that special bite. What an advantage that titmouse baby has, being guided through nature by his real parents.

Samson dropped to the ground occasionally, maintaining a closeness to me. I stood a moment to turn my chair a bit and immediately Samson came down to my shoulder as if to say, "Don't go."

Again, I conversed with him in whispers and he responded not. I asked him if he would go find Baby Sister. I asked him if she had run off with another little boy. He looked so little. He looked so forlorn. This was the longest he had ever stayed on my shoulder.

I tried not to read any meaning into it, but he knew and I knew, it was always Baby Sister who came to me first and lingered the longest.

When finally he flew to the overhead tree, he nestled there in the fork of two branches. Perhaps, my mind raced, that is what Baby Sister is doing somewhere in the forest, simply not ready to start her day. After all, yesterday was her first day of complete freedom and maybe she needs to sleep late after so much activity.

Samson dropped back onto the ground and again stayed too long. (Baby Sister is bad about that. I will not think about that. It is still early and she may be waiting until 7:00 a.m. to surprise me.)

Over and over in my mind came the picture of her chasing me yesterday afternoon, trying to get me to stand still for her to land. That was one of her cutest moments.

Samson glided to my chair and sat beside me.

An hour passed and he lifted to the branch above. I rose aimlessly and he came and sat on my arm. He tilted his little head to observe a tear fall beside him. There he lingered, looking sadly up into my face, soundless. Thirty more minutes passed, and suddenly I found myself pacing the grounds in search of Baby Sister, mechanically looking for any signs of her.

Samson followed my every step, hopping from branch to branch. We wound our way back to their home, where they had cuddled through their last night together. He sat on the roof for a while, then moved to the window ledge and looked into my face, then into their home, then back into my face.

How do I explain to him about loneliness? What do you say to a baby bluebird to make him understand his playmate is gone? The pain is too much, not for me, but for that little boy, alone for the first time, his sweet, faithful companion gone forever.

For the first time, he is not playful. All the other birds passing by travel in twos or in families, and Samson just stares, his eyes full of anguish.

Leaving him like that taunted me with grief, but

"For the first time, he is not playful . . . Samson just stares, his eyes full of anguish."

"He responded with light wing flutters but no sound and took little food. . . . How do I explain to him about loneliness? What do you say to a baby bluebird to make him understand . . . ?"

work responsibilities called me away. Tearfully, I tried to explain as gently as I could that I would have friends come sit under his tree and visit him through the day and nothing could stop me from hurrying home.

More fan mail arrived for Samson and Baby Sister today and little children asked about them all day. While gulping back tears, I repeatedly heard myself say, "Samson is hunting bugs in the trees and Baby Sister is free; she is forever free."

I do not remember driving home. I only remember a sick feeling. Quickly, Samson and I found each other. He met me soberly, still in quieted mood, and lethargically took food, still not uttering his sweet babyish delightful squeal just before each bite.

I lay on the lounge chair to be near him. Several times, he just came and sat on the top of my chair and I could feel him against my hair. Otherwise, he perched motionless overhead. I poured out the last of a box of crickets all over the ground and he showed interest only in one or two.

The bluebird adults brought their babies in and lined them in a row close by. Samson just observed in silence. If only they would befriend him.

At the last light of day and with the moon's reflection growing brighter, little Samson dropped onto my hand over my lap, looked up at me for a moment, then charged into the air and to the top of the antenna high over the roof top where he and Baby Sister played and played. Suddenly, he broke forth into forlorn calls, crying out again and again and again at the world as if crushed in anguish for his Baby Sister. These were the first sounds he had made in all these hours.

As quickly as he had risen to the roof top, he dropped into the bed of a tree against a barren limb and remained quiet. I tucked him in as lovingly as I knew how, my own voice quivering, and withdrew into my home.

DAY SIXTY

Thursday

Four a.m.: Last night's scene of Samson crying on the antenna jarred me into wakefulness, a sense of urgency compelling me to make contact with him. The forest remained in deep slumber. Nonetheless, I threw tender words up into the trees, then tiptoed back into my home. Sleep would not return. My mind got trapped on that treadmill of endless images that come on thought-crazed nights, with pictures of total joy and total despair warring with each other, the flickering back and forth tightening my neck in a tourniquet until my entire body lay stiffened. The weight of Samson's pitiful little face won out, drawing me back out into the dawn where I stood under the grandfather oak.

At 5:15 a.m., the sky streaked in gold on white, my baby blue boy dropped onto my arms. Again, he uttered no sounds. Continuously, I petted him with my voice, trying to nurse him into response. For ever so long, he moved from ground to branch to my shoulder, mute and mechanical. Was it wrong of me to believe that if he just could respond, he would feel better? Admittedly, that is the human way. Yet, he remained soundless.

At 7:45, the sun warmed the earth and promised a pleasant day. If Samson only could find more comfort in Mother Nature, but he takes his hurt to the only parent he has ever known and she cannot truly provide.

He fluttered onto my shoulder. Words poured out from my very soul, as if driven with a need to fill Samson's every cell with enough nourishment somehow to bring him back to life. I begged him to chirp. I begged him to coo. I begged him to tweet, to cry, to do anything, just to talk to me. I begged him to go forth and chase butterflies and slay dragons and mold castles in the clouds and do whatever he had to to get to next spring.

I told him his silence held such awful risks. If he did not respond, his heart surely would die. I told him if he just could stand up to the loneliness of the coming weeks, wondrous things awaited him.

He stood so still in his listening, studying my words, that I continued on in my babbling. I told him his life was as big and as meaningful as any king's, but if he remained silent, he would go unnoticed and suffer out a barren life of solitude. I told him how grand knowing Baby Sister had been and that I knew how much he hurt for her.

I pleaded with him to listen deep within, and all Baby Sister had been would get him to the other side of the winter, where he could take with him all his understanding of her vulnerability and her depth of loving to share with his own baby bluebirds. I told him if he could do this, he could make Baby Sister live forever through generations of bluebirds to come.

His eyes blinked and he tilted his head, but he made not one sound. Startling even to myself, suddenly in a whisper I began to sing, "Somewhere Over the Rainbow." He leaned into the air and glided into the grandfather oak. I tried to draw some humor from this, but a tear came instead.

As the morning aged, Samson sat motionless in resignation when I was forced to leave for work. Human children had calls on me, too. I walked through the day like a stick figure, the mental images from 4:00 that morning keeping a vise on my mood.

Driving back onto home grounds closer to Samson late in the evening brought some relief, but try as I might, I could not find beauty in the splendor of the moonlit night. The burden of damming up tears so long had been exhausting. I wanted to cry out for Samson, but neither of us made a sound.

DAY SIXTY-ONE

Friday

Two-fifteen a.m.: Crackling of thunder slapped me into consciousness, warning me of potential danger. I awoke and discovered a pillow wet with tears.

The wrecking winds last week reportedly mounted an unnumbered death toll of fledgling baby birds, downing branches, massive trees, and power lines over the entire area. With concern for my own safety, there was that tiny boy alone outside.

Through others of these storms, the shelter of Samson's home had protected him, his Baby Sister holding tightly against his side to share his fears. He had been yanked by his frail baby neck to the door of his nesting box by nature gone wild, and flung from his parents onto the cold ground seven feet below, and survived. At five days old, with blood speckling the corner of his broken mouth, he had lain next to his dying siblings and survived. He had withstood the repeated onslaughts of those adult bluebirds. He had experienced the loss of his baby sister and carried the burden of grief alone. And now, without explanation, he was expected to bend to the ground with trees tossed by violent winds. How much can one small bird—or one small boy—endure?

Friends have asked why I did not merely bring him inside and guarantee his safety. Cage this valiant little knight? What of life's meaning could a cage bring a bluebird? If only he can endure nature's dumbfounding blows, I prayed, surely next spring will bring explanation enough.

At 4:00 a.m., the earth quieted but my head would

not. Again, the torturous images fettered my mind, now adding pictures of a wind-beaten, bereft Samson alone outside. By 5:45, the rain turned into mist that captured the sun's first reflections, casting glittery light rays all about my face.

As I moved out across the sun deck, scanning the scene below, I saw the injury to the grandfather oak. Its most massive arm was broken, lying sadly over the baby birds' graves. I, too, wanted to climb to the top of the antenna and screech out forlorn cries at the world.

A little blue-winged boy landed on my arm and stopped me. His eyes, very wide, looked as if they had seen hell. He seemed resigned to what nature could do to the most meek and magnificent of its beings. His deepening blue coat was flecked with the glittery mist but the contrast between the sparkling of his beautiful colorings and the sadness of his expression only intensified my anguish for him.

As he crouched lower and lower on my shoulder, he leaned into me and I was glad. I sighed that breath of deliverance, so relieved to see he had lasted out another of these battering storms. Spawned by the kind of determination that sometimes intensifies with fatigue and strain, I was sworn to break this agonizing silence. This was the battle cry for the day and I was prepared to pay any ransom for this battered infant's freedom.

My lips parted and a well of soft-toned dialogue seemed to find its own course. "Sweet, sweet, Samson," I pleaded, "let me be your haven. I'll greet you every morning and we can play together all summer."

I told him he could sit by my fire through the winter and pull worms from my garden in the spring. I told him I would pick mulberries and freeze them for him to eat one by one each winter's day, and we could titter when all the other birds wondered why he had mulberry juice on his chin. I told him that sometimes we could sit in his birdhouse if he ever needed to and talk about Baby Sister and look at her pictures. I told him we could paint a nail keg like a cricket box and chase each other around it until no more tag was left in us.

Dawn passed into day and Samson remained with me, somber and inanimate, his eyes dulled and lifeless. Yet he listened. I was prepared to stand there until the sun deck rotted.

On and on and on I spoke. I told him over and over that I loved him. I told him that I would wear my big fuzzy coat on cold winter days and he could nestle down in my collar, as Baby Sister had against him, and in the spring, a pretty little girl would come along to be his fuzzy coat.

He lifted slightly and shifted his head. My voice growing gravelish, the sun beginning to burn the back of my knees, and my neck stiffening, I paused, ready to break into nursery rhymes.

In the hush, I thought I heard a whimpered coo. The dog's barking at horses down the road broke the spell and Samson fluttered to be with the grandfather oak. I called to him my pledge for the day and hobbled stifflegged off the sun deck.

Perfumed breezes nudged morning on into afternoon and the day warmed without awareness. Periodically, Samson dropped to the bird bath for water. Repeatedly, he seemed to lose track of time and just sat on the edge of the tiny pool, staring into the liquid. Perhaps he saw the same reflection as I . . . of Baby Sister. He hopped once into the bowl and half-heartedly dipped his head, then lifted off to a branch to dry. More often, he came to my lap and just stared blankly into space or watched my face. Each time, I talked and talked and talked to him. His silence grew heavier. I felt so inadequate.

Shadows grew on the ground and the air filled with the moist aroma of the evening. I moved toward the water faucet and, with hose in hand, sprayed from one side of the grounds to the other.

Samson glided from leaf to limb fluttering in and out of my lengthening shadow. My mind adrift, my mouth muttering, I was unaware of the increasing volume in my voice in keeping contact with Samson. He had held his distance as I lumbered over to give the cherry tree a drink. At first, I wondered if Samson was napping. Then I understood. The cherry tree was next to Samson's and Baby Sister's home.

I suddenly realized that more and more, he had avoided nearing the birdhouse. The water splashing on the ground felt like tears, as I hastened to Samson's side, away from the home of joyful play once upon a time a century ago. For an hour, I joined Samson in the oppressive silence, my soul searching for answers, faced with the fact that if the trance could not be shattered, there would be no spring.

The sky's blues gave way to brilliant orange, telling me my pledge for the day was in jeopardy. Like a runner's sprint in the final lap, the threat charged me on, doubling my energies and supply of dialogue. Samson came immediately to my shoulder for more as I began again, now as if to encourage me. I wanted to kiss the tiny blue feather scarcely peeking through the gray over his beak.

Softly, I shared splendid scenes of him in the spring. I told him how much I loved him and how we could stay side by side through the months to come, and how much I knew a little bluebird girl would love him and how they

"When his cheek touched mine, something wonderful happened."

"That incredible little creature . . . spread his wings over the water . . . Samson finally accepted the baptism of life."

would have the sweetest babies ever to peek out of an aqua blue egg.

Hours of minutes passed as my words spun into the evening air. On and on I continued, turning my head farther and farther in his direction. When his cheek touched mine, something wonderful happened. Samson reached out and slightly pulled at my hair. I held breathlessly still. So much in tune with his silence, I felt I could hear his heart beat.

In the midst of the pause, he whimpered. I broke into oratory, poetry, anything—the words tumbling out trying to strengthen him. Another whimper, this time a little stronger, as if urging me to continue. He cooed. I tried to coo. He chirped. I think I chirped. He tweeted. I know I tweeted. And away we went, back and forth, each egging the other on.

We were the debate at the United Nations, classmates at a reunion, Abbott and Costello, Chip and Dale, and on and on we chattered. Mine was joyful jabber. His was surrender into freedom. My sick child's fever was broken. Feeling began to return to the back of my neck. In the pause it took to complete a grin, his volume increased, pushing me on for more. I gave him all he wanted, jabber for jabber.

My need to ring bells, to squeal, to celebrate, to do something grand lifted me from the chair, Samson on my shoulder. With an air of pomp and circumstance, I filled the birdbath.

That incredible little creature on my shoulder spread his wings over the water and hopped into the cool liquid. Covering his beautiful body again and again, Samson washed away the risks of silence, finally accepting the baptism of life. He lifted to a branch to groom himself as I slumped back into the lounge chair, the Hallelujah Chorus ringing in my ears.

"I smiled the smile only proud parents can smile and told him he was wonderful. He sat on my shoulder, gazing into the sunset, a new brightness in his eyes."

But the music had only just begun. Samson, all fluffy and shiny from his bath, dropped down on my arm for inspection. He was at that gawky but gorgeous stage, appearing babyish one minute and maturing adolescent the next, a regular little teenager. No sooner had he settled on my arm than the air filled with the whisperings of bluebirds, a family of seven, two parents and five offspring only a few days from Samson's age. All cascaded downward and onto the antenna. The adults took positions toward the back to guard their five young ones who gathered across the broader antenna ribs. Precisely on the point, most prim and proper, perched a dainty, cuddly little girl, peering out to the north in our direction.

I felt Samson's body lift as his eyes caught hers. He darted straight for the antenna. The parents made a half-hearted attempt to shoo him away, but boldly Samson stood his ground, winding up on the side rib, not eighteen inches from the little girl, looking directly at her.

Samson and the little girl filled my binoculars with the story that began a million years ago . . . boy and girl. She ducked her head, then slowly turned her face in his direction, as coy as any female since the beginning of time.

Flirtatiously, she lifted her head towards him, setting him into spasms of chatter.

My mind provided the dialogue: "My name's Samson. I'm seven weeks old. I live here. You want to play? What's your name? I had a baby sister, but she died. You like mulberries? Want to see my birdhouse?"

The little girl studied him, tilting her head impishly, then the family lifted toward the sunset, Samson, too. He fluttered by the baby girl's side to the edge of the grandfather oak, then returned to tell me, his mama, all about it.

Yes, I told him, I had seen the little girl. I smiled the smile only proud parents can smile and told him he was wonderful. He sat on my shoulder, gazing into the sunset, a new brightness in his eyes.

This baby boy, thrown into life, nourished by an Easter egg, who suffered death and despair from nature's crucifying blows, now was resurrected. A new blue feather colored his wing, God's promise to clothe this tiny son in His finest.

It was there I willed Samson all my earth, to build his home, his mate inseparable beside him.

Samson had been correctly christened. Samson was a tough little bird.

I told him I could see the sky-blue eggs that would come in the springtime, with tough little Samsons crawling out, kingborn, squealing for food, ready to plunge into life, and their father, Samson, with the wisdom of Job, there proudly to protect them and to share all the special things that had been Baby Sister.

He leaned into me and touched my cheek.

EPILOGUE

During the following days, I told Samson I would write his and Baby Sister's story, and proved it by sitting hour after hour on the floor of my bedroom with my back against the wall under the open window. He whiled away his time along the window sill or on the frame holding the metal fireplace chimney just outside.

We called back and forth to each other as I wrote. He hopped onto my shoulder and toyed with my hair or held still to study the new surroundings inside my bedroom.

Our mornings were special. We would start very early, Samson, the water hose, and I. From the first-story roof ledge, he watched for worms as I moved inch-by-inch around the house spraying water on the grass.

Then one day, Samson did not meet me at my window, nor on my lounge chair, nor did he chase insects fleeing from my water hose. I told myself he had gone to ford rivers and build castles in the sky and to seek his fortune. Determinedly, I refused to think of cats or snakes or marauding hawks. Lonely, worried days passed. My window remained open.

Then, one morning I thought I heard bluebirds on the antenna. A rush outside did not prove me right. Back inside, I still thought I heard bluebirds but another run failed to prove me right. Again, back inside I knew I heard bluebirds. I began to wonder if so many weeks with baby bluebirds had begun to do something to me. I moved up the stairway thinking this thought, and stopped short.

There on the curtain rod over our special window sat my baby boy. He had come home for his mulberry allowance and some home cooking—and had brought his little girlfriend with him. She was trapped inside the third floor crow's nest and was scared to death.

Easily I freed her, and we became friends. I named her Petals because she was so pretty and had just floated in. Her wings were whiter than other bluebirds', as I had noticed through my binoculars on the evening Samson had introduced himself to her. Perhaps she had a bit of angel in her. They stayed awhile. We played and talked. And then, side by side, they left.

A few days later, I was at another place on my land about a mile away and was talking to a man about some business matters. All of a sudden Samson and Petals appeared on the telephone wire. Down the fence line were Petal's four siblings. No adults accompanied them and I concluded the parents were involved in their last nesting. It was the right time of year.

Samson, acting so excited to see me, chirped and tweeted, and as I began to chirp and twitter in reply and talk baby talk to a little bluebird overhead, I am not sure the man did not think I was a little strange. But then, when Samson came down to say hello and sat on my shoulder and I introduced them, I am positive he did.

As the weeks wore on, Samson's outings and returnings grew further and further apart until, finally, one day he did not return.

Except for days of snow or driving rains, my bedroom window remained open for Samson.

It was Friday, and I had not seen him for a year and two days. I had just topped the stairs and turned into my bedroom. Suddenly, many blue wings began to flutter down onto the power wire just outside the window. Samson and Petals had returned, and they were covered up with babies.

"Sam-son! Sup-pa-time," I whispered instinctively. I knew if I moved, I would frighten the eleven little ones, and so he came to me on the window sill. He waved his wings in a fluttering hello and chirped eagerly. I had not spoken baby bluebird talk for a year, and it felt good.

He was magnificent, and I wondered if his coat was a lighter sky-blue than other male bluebirds because he had been raised on a different diet. I chose to believe he was more beautiful because he was Samson.

His youngsters would not hold still long for a visit with grandmother and lifted toward the front of the house. Samson lingered a moment, then joined his family. I ran automatically to the freezer and took out a tiny patty of his homemade recipe. Keeping food ready somehow kept me feeling prepared for Samson's return.

In 90 seconds, I had the food defrosted in the micro-wave and into the same little eating cup, a toothpick in hand, and was back at the bedroom window. There I knelt with food on the toothpick as if the last feeding had been only an hour earlier, poised and ready in hopes that very little movement would be necessary on my part should Samson return.

In another 90 seconds, Samson landed not six inches from my hand and, as we had a thousand times or more, we responded to each other naturally and he took the food. I displayed my instinct, but he did, too, and hopped to the wire to share the bite with his tiniest baby girl who nibbled her first taste of grandma's cooking, then leaned into her father as Baby Sister had done to her big brother.

I wondered if Samson had taught her to do this. He fed her easily with his curved beak, laying to rest one of the final mysteries about Samson I had held for a year in my mind, for I had wondered how he would manage to feed his offspring with his misshapen bill. In another moment, he lifted toward the north, twelve pairs of bluebird wings following him.

I slid down the stairs and snatched up the camera. Out the back door I galloped, hesitating only when I discovered what Samson was doing. He was showing his family his home, and his babies were crawling all over it. The aviary was filled with weeds and a rain-filled water bowl. A discolored cricket box lay in one corner. Brittle mulberry branches, dead and lifeless, hung from the walls.

The memory flooded back of how painful Baby Sister's death had been. Until now, neither Samson nor I had neared the aviary after those final hours searching for her little body. Now, I believed I could dismantle that once little magic cottage on the edge of the forest and preserve it, perhaps for another Samson and Baby Sister.

I stood five feet from the sweetgum tree, just below one of Samson's favorite evening feeding branches. He came to me and I got to tell him again how much I loved him and how proud of him I was. This was my Easter egg boy, and he had returned, bringing with him new life. Petals remained on the aviary with their brood.

Then, Samson in the lead, all lifted toward the north and back to the west beyond the grandfather oak.

A week later, Samson brought his kids to play on the antenna, a kind of romp at grandma's house before bedtime. He came down from the platform on the little windmill to say hello and two of his offspring tried to follow him, but they hesitated with me so close and returned to their mama on the antenna, where Samson initially had met his bride. Petals surveyed the situation from the back of the antenna where her parents had sat when Samson introduced himself.

After the antenna had had a good workout, Samson gathered up his family in the grandfather oak and bedded them down above his brothers' and sisters' little graves. I arose at 4:30 a.m., and waited. At 5:15, Samson landed close to my feet on the lounge chair and we talked for a while before the children awoke. Soon the family stirred and Samson gathered them to him and led them into the dawn. And so the story continues.

For the rest of my life, when I see a bluebird in the spring, I will wonder if it is my grandson, or great-granddaughter, or great-great-grandchild. . .

Two years and two months from Samson's birth, it was Petal's soft cries that awakened me. Baby whispers echoed hers. The cool spring morning and aroma of honeysuckle that hung in a halo overhead reminded me of those wonderful days in the aviary. The earth was so silent it tugged at my attention.

I found Petals on the nesting box at the finger tips of the grandfather oak. Her mourning mood and muted cries told me to scan the skies for Samson as I had for Baby Sister. This time I did not pace the grounds. I simply stood and stared in Petal's direction, trying to understand the meaning of her flights back and forth from the grandfather oak to the nesting box.

Petals was telling me to come to the nesting box. She lifted to the grandfather oak beside her babies as I lifted the lid of my baby boy's coffin. Samson had come home to die. His magnificent body lay as if sleeping in a newly started nest of pine straw. It was our first greeting in which he did not flutter his wings in gleeful delight. I cupped the nest holding my tiny son, and walked with it next to my heart to the graves of his brothers and sisters. I talked to him as I prepared his little grave. Petals and her children sat quietly overhead.

As I gave my brave little bluebird back to the earth, I rubbed my finger down his little crooked beak and said a prayer of thanksgiving. As I took the little blue feather from the side of the nest and tucked it in my denim pocket over my heart, I could feel his spirit meet Baby Sister's, and all creatures who ever knew freedom.

I went to my bedroom and closed the window, knowing only a little lift would reopen it. I had chosen to get involved.

Through the glass I could see a baby bluebird boy studying my movements from the power pole. It was one of Samson's sons.

ABOUT THE AUTHOR

Dr. Shirl Brunell is indeed a Renaissance Woman.

Born and raised in Alamogordo, New Mexico, she had her first major success when she triumphed over the handicap of being a learning disabled child to become a National Honor Student.

Then, in the 1950's, while an undergraduate of the University of New Mexico and later Woodbury College and UCLA, she was crowned Miss California College Queen of America and Miss New Mexico Maid of Cotton. Later, as one of the West Coast's busiest models, she was seen in print and on television as the Lee Rider Blue Jeans Girl, Borden's Milk Girl, and Plaid Trading Stamp Girl, and modeled for such diversified sponsors as Chevrolet, Cole of California Swimsuits, and Tareyton Cigarettes. She also was one of the hostesses on Queen For A Day and appeared on The Ernie Kovacs Show.

But her desire to work with emotionally disturbed adults and children outweighed the glamorous life, and in the mid-sixties, she returned to school, where she earned her Doctorate with Honors in Psychology at the University of Houston. Today, in addition to being one of America's most respected clinical psychologists and authorities on the treatment of children and abused women, she is a renowned naturalist and prizewinning photographer.

A resident of Texarkana, USA, she has been a

staff psychologist at the Veterans Administration Hospital in Houston, Texas, the Houston Medical Center, and a member of various government and professional boards and councils, including the Arkansas State Council for the Prevention of Juvenile Delinquency.

When not consulting at the Texarkana Mental Health and Mental Retardation Center or not involved with her private practice, Dr. Brunell spends her time writing, photographing and observing nature, or playing the musical saw.

The extenuating circumstances that led to the hand raising of Samson and Baby Sister hopefully will in no way encourage anyone to attempt a similar experience, except under comparable dire circumstances. It is unlawful to hand raise any native wild bird and a federal permit is required to do so. A license may be obtained through the nearest district office of the UNITED STATES FISH AND WILDLIFE SERVICE, LAW ENFORCEMENT DIVISION, U. S. DEPARTMENT OF THE INTERIOR.

The sow bug, roly-poly "chocolate" morsel, pill bug given to Samson and Baby Sister has been found to carry a parasite that potentially could be deadly to the bluebird. Therefore, this is not recommended as a food source. Also, I more recently learned that any 100% complete and balanced high quality canned dog food provides adequate nourishment for many birds, including the bluebird, in an emergency.

Dr. Lawrence Zeleny's book *The Bluebird, How You Can Help Its Fight For Survival,* published for the Audubon Naturalist Society of the Central Atlantic States by Indiana University Press and obtained through the North American Bluebird Society, Box 6295, Silver Spring. MD 20906, is an invaluable resource in a bluebird emergency.

Dr. Shirl Brunell